Cris Rogers is a Church of England church planter, artist and *Star Wars* fan. In 2010, Cris and his family moved to Tower Hamlets, one of the toughest boroughs in east London, and took on the leadership of All Hallows, Bow. The desire was to restart the church, which had shrunk to seven members, and see people flourish. Cris has a deep passion for discipleship and this desire, with the support of the team and community, is being realized. Cris also runs the weekly podcast 'Making Disciples with Cris Rogers' and wider ministry that is Making Disciples, which can be found online at <wearemakingdisciples.com>.

GW00372207

CRIS ROGERS

APPRENTICE TO JESUS

40 DAYS OF WALKING IN THE WAY

First published in Great Britain in 2020

Society for Promoting Christian Knowledge
36 Causton Street
London SW1P 4ST
www.spck.org.uk

The author and publisher have made every effort to ensure that the external website and
email addresses included in this book are correct and up to date at the time of going
to press. The author and publisher are not responsible for the content, quality or
continuing accessiblility of the sites.

Unless otherwise noted, Scripture quotations are taken from The Holy Bible,
New International Version (Anglicized edition). Copyright © 1979, 1984, 2011 by Biblica.
Used by permission of Hodder & Stoughton Ltd, an Hachette UK company. All rights
reserved. 'NIV' is a registered trademark of Biblica. UK trademark number 1448790.

Scripture quotations marked ESV are taken from The Holy Bible, English Standard
Version, copyright © 2001 by Crossway, a publishing ministry of Good News Publishers.
Used by permission. All rights reserved.

Scripture quotations marked NLT are from the *Holy Bible*, New Living Translation,
copyright © 1996, 2004, 2015 by Tyndale House Foundation. Used by permission of
Tyndale House Publishers, Inc., Carol Stream, Illinois 60188. All rights reserved.

Scripture quotations marked NRSV are from the New Revised Standard Version of the
Bible, Anglicized Edition, copyright © 1989, 1995 by the Division of Christian Education
of the National Council of the Churches of Christ in the USA. Used by permission.
All rights reserved.

Every effort has been made to seek permission to use copyright material reproduced in
this book. The publisher apologizes for those cases where permission might not have been
sought and, if notified, will formally seek permission at the earliest opportunity.

British Library Cataloguing-in-Publication Data
A catalogue record for this book is available from the British Library

ISBN 978–0–281–07998–8
eBook ISBN 978–0–281–08503–3

1 3 5 7 9 10 8 6 4 2

Typeset by Manila Typesetting Company
First printed in Turkey by Elma Basim

eBook by Manila Typesetting Company

Produced on paper from sustainable forests

CONTENTS

CONTENTS

FOREWORD

Does my life look like that of Jesus and, if not, how do I get there? These two powerful questions set the tone for everything you are about to read from Cris and members of his church at All Hallows, Bow, in east London. This book is insightfully built around the idea of apprenticeship.

Apprenticeships have recaptured the public mind in recent years. They have been touted as an alternative professional pathway to deal with issues of unemployment and lack of skills. Although they may be benefiting from a new push, apprenticeships are, in fact, ancient. They have, for centuries, been an invaluable means of gaining skills on the job. In this series of forty reflections, we are reminded that followers of Jesus should consider themselves as enrolled apprentices. Just as the aim of apprentices is to learn the ways of their teacher, so the aim of Christians is to learn the ways of Jesus. The apostle Paul states it simply in his first letter to the Corinthians: 'Be imitators of me, as I am of Christ' (1 Corinthians 11.1 NRSV).

True to the central premise of apprenticeship, this book is intensely focused on making progress along the way. It constantly encourages us to move from a passive mode of mere listening to an active mode of learning that helps us in practical ways to develop and to grow. Each reflection is rooted in Scripture and wonderfully applied. As you engage in the reflective exercises, answer questions and wrestle with God in prayer, the aim is that you will experience the Spirit's work in a new way.

FOREWORD

The recent history of apprenticeships in London is fascinating. Dr Patrick Wallis, from the London School of Economics, has written that apprenticeships 'made the capital into the largest educational site that existed in England before compulsory basic schooling was introduced in the late nineteenth century. The share of the population who were trained in the city exceeded the proportion going to university before the 1980s.' I dare to pray for even bigger results from Christ's apprentices in our great city and around the world today. May this resource be part of the way that God enables everyone to encounter the love of God in Christ.

Without doubt, anyone who embarks on this forty-day journey will be challenged, changed and better equipped to serve the Church and bring glory to God in the years ahead.

The Rt Revd and Rt Hon. Dame Sarah Mullally DBE

THANKS

This book started first as a short one written by members of All Hallows Church, Bow, east London, where I am the pastor. The best bits were written by others and the sketchy bits probably by me. Huge thanks to the members of All Hallows who helped to shape the early drafts of this book: Beki, Dan, Ellie, Franzi, Alex, Raff, Esther, Flick, Robbie, Tom and Ed.

INTRODUCTION

Does my life look like that of Jesus?

This is the question we, as disciples, should be asking ourselves daily. If we were to compare our lives with that of Jesus, how closely would they be aligned? Can others recognize Jesus in us? Are we Christlike? These questions aren't meant to make any one of us feel guilty; they should *inspire* us.

We are each invited to grow and mature into the likeness of Jesus but, if you were to ask many of us, we would admit that we struggle to see ourselves doing so in the way we would hope. The Bible models disciples as being more like apprentices than simply being learners. Discipleship in the Way of Jesus isn't about learning what Jesus knew, it's about being like, and doing the work of, Jesus. Jesus called each of us into the 'Jesus movement' to become carriers of his message and of his power in action.

Why is it that so many older Sunday school teachers have this beautiful aroma of Jesus about them? Is it because they have spent so many years teaching the simplicity of the gospel? Is it because they too have learned to come to Jesus like children? Is it because, during those years of investing in others, they have marinated in Jesus' love? Is it because they are always working out what faith looks like on the ground?

The answer is probably all of these things. If, over time, we continue to invest in our relationship with Jesus and commit each day to behaving like he did, then we will naturally become more like him.

In the Bible, the number 40 signifies a pivotal moment. Each time we see this number in the Bible, we witness someone starting in one place but ending in a better one. The people of God were led in the wilderness for 40 years; Jesus fasted and was tempted for 40 days. Forty days is a significant amount of time to commit to God and for God to commit to his people.

While journeying through these 40 daily topics and thoughts, let's discover practices that will unlock faith and life in abundance for each of us. Imagine what it would be like if, in 40 days, we were to look back and see dramatic growth and increased connection with God. What if we were able to invest in our relationship with him, and to start to look, act and be like Jesus?

WORKING OUT YOUR SHAPE

Before we look at our daily material, let's first reflect on how our faith currently is. Jesus wants to shape all aspects of our lives but, without good probing questions, it's easy to overlook areas that Jesus would like to influence. We're going to start by simply filling in a 20-question assessment tool. This disciple-making tool (see pages 6–8) helps us to take time to review honestly each part of our lives. The tool's questions are personal and community-related, and focus on the areas of the head, heart and hands.

WHY FOCUS ON THE HEAD, HEART AND HANDS?

Jesus was approached one day and asked, 'Which is the greatest commandment?' He responded, '"Love the Lord your God with all your heart and with all your soul and with all your strength and with all your mind"; and, "Love your neighbour as yourself"' (Luke 10.27).

We're to *love God with our hearts, our souls, our strength and our minds.* Taking this call to give ourselves fully to Christ, the disciple-making tool provides questions to reflect on and respond to. It teaches us to become disciples, exploring areas of potential. Personal discipleship is about moving closer to what Jesus wants for us in every area of our lives. This has been broken down into three areas – our **heads**, **hearts** and **hands**.

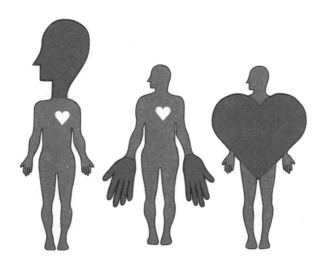

Disciples of Jesus are called to use their minds (heads) to grow in knowledge of him; to be filled with desire and passion for him in their hearts; and to use their hands to be active in serving him. However, many disciples can be overdeveloped in one area and underdeveloped in another. We can end up with big heads and hearts but small hands, or big hearts but small heads and hands. Our challenge is to understand ourselves and to seek to invest in areas of our lives other than the dominant ones. It can be good to play to our strengths, but when it comes to discipleship we need to be balanced in all areas.

Conversation and reflection are encouraged in conjunction with using the disciple-making tool. The tool can be used in a large church setting, a smaller home group setting or a one-to-one with a trusted, more mature Christian or mentor. It helps to reveal each individual's personal 'shape'. When used in a larger group setting, it can also reveal the shape of the group or even a church. From areas that are identified using the tool, a mentor can help the user to see some ways in which he or she might develop.

Make yourself some coffee, sit in a quiet corner and go through the 20 questions in the disciple-making tool, starting on the next page, answering them slowly. The worksheet is not only provided here but also at <https://wearemakingdisciples.com>, where you can assess yourself on the website and save your results for future review.

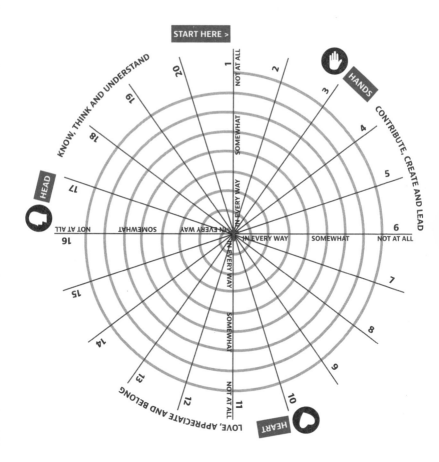

QUESTIONS TO CONSIDER

On each of the 40 days we spend together in this book, we will reflect on one or more of the 20 questions in the disciple-making tool and complete an activity. We will look at each question from two different angles to help create a pattern of probing. We won't look at them in the order given here; the aim is to explore aspects of the head, heart and hands as a whole.

As you answer each of the following questions, make a little pencil dot at a point along the line in the diagram, left, to give your answer – 'in every way', 'somewhat' or 'not at all'. For question 1, put your dot on the line with '1' at the end and continue to work your way clockwise round the circle.

1 How much of your day-to-day life changes as you think about what it means to live for Jesus?
2 How committed are you to a local church community?
3 How much would you say your faith leads you to serve and care for others?
4 To what extent are you helping others to serve God better?
5 How willing are you to put in place helpful boundaries?
6 To what extent are you serving Jesus in collaboration with others?
7 How much are your daily habits changing to reflect God's care for his creation?
8 How much does tragedy and injustice in the world move you to action?
9 How engaged are you in a personal and community prayer life?
10 To what extent are you completely open and honest with one or two close friends about your strengths and failings?
11 To what extent are areas of sin and brokenness in your life being changed by Jesus?
12 To what extent is your relationship with God being regularly cultivated and deepened?
13 To what extent is your heart in line with God's love and desire?

14 How much of an impact do your beliefs and the Bible have on your attitude towards culture, the world and your community?

15 Are you open to wrestling with and being challenged about things you believe?

16 To what extent are you allowing yourself to learn from those who think differently from you?

17 How much time do you regularly spend engaging with the Bible?

18 To what extent are you regularly discovering more about Jesus and his work in our world?

19 How often do you regularly discuss your faith with others?

20 To what extent does your reading of the Bible point you towards Jesus and how to live for him?

Disciples of Jesus are called to use their minds (heads) to grow in knowledge of him; to be filled with desire and passion for him in their hearts; and to use their hands to be active in serving him. However, many disciples can be overdeveloped in one area and underdeveloped in another. We can end up with big heads and hearts but small hands, or big hearts but small heads and hands. Our challenge is to understand ourselves and seek to invest in areas of our lives other than the dominant ones. It can be good to play to our strengths but, when it comes to discipleship, we need to be balanced in all areas.

If you have answered the questions in the disciple-making tool honestly and joined the dots you have made on the lines of the wheel on page 6, you will now have a shape. The shape indicates your passions and biases. The nearer the centre of the disciple-making tool your answers are, the greater the strength indicated; the nearer the edges your answers are, the more you need to work on and invest in those areas. It is likely that you have one or two areas that are stronger than others. This isn't a problem – it's an exciting opportunity. We all have aspects that are stronger, and in which we are more active, and others that are less so. Jesus wants to transform all areas of our lives.

You might find it helpful to discuss your answers and your shape with a friend or a mature Christian you trust. He or she can help you to find ways to strengthen those areas that need work.

First, choose which shape best matches your own.

 The **bean** shape indicates that one area is more developed than the other two. This might reveal a headstrong personality, for which the heart and hands are less developed. It might also show a compassionate and active faith, but one that lacks a strong biblical foundation. It is easy to allow our preferences to develop at the expense of other areas. Can you identify the areas that are weaker and need more attention?

 The **pear** shape shows that one area of the three is less developed than the other two. Ask yourself why that might be. Have you neglected this area or have you lacked the opportunity to develop it?

 The **larger circle** indicates little confidence in all three areas, which is exciting! It means you have an adventure ahead. You can build up all the areas to become balanced and engaged. You might like to ask someone trustworthy if he or she thinks that this shape truly reflects you. Often others see strengths that we overlook.

 The **pea** shape reflects a rounded, balanced kind of discipleship. Head, heart and hands all work well together. The challenge here is to sustain commitment. Usually, the more people know Christ, the more they realize that they don't have it all together. How do you keep developing and growing? Is there anyone with whom you can be completely honest? Can he or she identify any weak areas of growth in you?

The **starfish** outline is less clear. All three areas are inconsistent within themselves. The shape indicates that although you are moving towards Jesus in some ways, you need to invest in other areas. It is worth flagging the questions answered 'NOT AT ALL' to see if there's a link between them. Often, a connection between marks at the centre of the tool, or between those on the edge, may be apparent. The commonality might concern issues such as commitment, daily rhythms, working with others, and private and public life.

THE SPIRAL

Did you notice the spiral in the background of the diagram on page 6? We often think of our journey with Jesus as one of walking forwards on a long road. In reality, however, the same issues surface time and time again. The journey of discipleship is more like a spiral. The question is, are we moving towards or away from Jesus? When a familiar problem resurfaces, do we handle things differently? Are we behaving better than before? Are we more Christlike now?

Naturally, the questions in the disciple-making tool aren't ones that we ask only once and then forget about; these are questions that we have to ask ourselves again and again. This is only the beginning of a much longer and continuous process. This process could be hard but hopefully it will also be fun. Discipleship in the Way of Jesus should be fun and never done on our own. The Holy Spirit is there to counsel us through this process. At all points, it is good practice to invite the Spirit to be with us and speak to us. The Spirit comes to challenge us and to encourage each of us. He is also the Great Healer, who heals our wounds and brings full restoration.

LIVING FOR JESUS, NOT JUST READING OF JESUS

Q. 17: How much time do you regularly spend engaging with the Bible?

As for what was sown on good soil, this is the one who hears the word and understands it. He indeed bears fruit and yields, in one case a hundredfold, in another sixty, and in another thirty.
(Matthew 13.23 ESV)

I'm not the keenest of gardeners. I've grown vegetables but I enjoy eating them far more. What I do know is that seeds by themselves don't have the potential for becoming something beautiful. It is the planting of and investing in them, making sure that they have rich soil and are well watered, that helps them to grow and produce fruit. The same can be said of the seeds of the gospel we find in the Bible. We shouldn't just read the Bible; we should also allow it to germinate and grow in us.

I've been a disciple who has devoted about 24 years of my life to Jesus. In that time, I've had seasons during which I've really invested in reading the Bible and other seasons less so. As each year passes, and my understanding and knowledge of Jesus develops, I've started to see deeper and deeper truths and patterns in the Bible that germinate and grow in me. The more I feed on the Bible, the more fruit I see in my life. Knowledge in itself is helpful but it can make us historians of Jesus, rather than disciples, unless we allow it to transform our lives. For many years in the Church, it has commonly been said:

> If we have the word of God without the Spirit of
> God: we dry up;
> if we have the Spirit of God without the word of
> God: we blow up;
> but if we have the word of God and the Spirit of
> God: we grow up.

The Franciscan friar Richard Rohr writes in his blog, *Belief or Discipleship*, that

> we do not think ourselves into a new way of living, but we live ourselves into a new way of thinking. I'm not suggesting that theory and theology are unimportant; but I believe that faith is more about how we live on a daily basis . . . [M]y life's work . . . has been trying to move heady doctrines and dogmas to the level of actual experience and lifestyles.

The question is, are we willing to activate the teachings and life of Jesus in our lives? Doing so may cause people to look at us and think for a moment that they are with Jesus himself.

Incorporating what we learn about Jesus into a living experience can be a challenge. Sometimes we might not see the connection between Jesus' world and ours. In such a moment, we may just have to take a step back to look at the bigger picture.

The Bible tells us that Jesus fed 5,000 people. Although we might not ever face a catering challenge that large, we might have a 'faith-needs-expanding' situation in our lives. Every passage of the Bible has many applications because the Holy Spirit will reveal to each of us different truths that are applicable to our own unique situations.

There are several ways of activating the teaching of the Bible, but the easiest is simply to pause and take a moment to pray. Ask the Holy Spirit to speak to you through the passage as you read it. Once you have done so, ask yourself 'What is God showing me through this passage? What is jumping out at me?'

Many passages are stories told with a principle to learn or to activate in our lives. These stories help us to see humanity's failings and God's actions. Some are direct teachings that simply have to be applied. Sometimes a passage declares a truth about God, and the appropriate response is to allow this truth to shape how we see him and wonder at his power and might.

YES, BUT HOW?

Taking the teachings of Jesus and activating them in our day-to-day lives requires us to ask questions of ourselves. Each day, I start by taking a short, focused retreat (with a cup of coffee and my Bible in a quiet corner and hitting pause). We can be so consumed by the present that we forget to focus on the eternal. Try taking a six-minute retreat that will help to build your relationship with God (see the 3-2-1 daily retreat overleaf). It is this daily rhythm that not only sustains us but also transforms us into the likeness of Jesus.

THREE MINUTES: BIBLE

Take out your Bible – either a printed or a digital one.

Read a short passage, bit by bit, to allow yourself to take it in. If this is your first time reading the Bible, a good place to start is with a Gospel, followed by the book called the Acts of the Apostles (or, simply, Acts). Alternatively, read a passage from a Bible study guide or start with a Bible structured to be read in a year (for example, *The Bible in One Year* (New International Version)).

As you read the short passage, ask yourself these three questions.

1 What does this tell me about God?
2 What does this tell me about me?
3 What can I do to live out what I've read?

TWO MINUTES: PRAY

Either in your mind or out loud, simply say what is happening in your life.

Give thanks in addition to sharing your needs. You can start by saying something simple such as 'Hello, God', 'Dear Father God' or 'God, come and find me'. Then just go for it.

ONE MINUTE: LISTEN

God wants to talk to you, as well as listen. Take a moment to listen to him too. Sometimes you might get a sense of what he is saying. Some people experience an emotion; you might just feel his presence. This is all positive and part of knowing God. If you hear or feel nothing, don't worry. Sit still with God. When you are ready to end, say 'Amen' (which means 'so be it').

After each six-minute retreat, you might like to try to set a goal to try to live out the revealed truth from the passage. Goals should be SMART: Specific, Measurable, Achievable, Relevant and Time-bound.* This way we know what we are going to try, how it relates to our lives and when we have done it.

---

* Specific (something clear that you know you can do); Measurable (something that you can see you have completed); Achievable (something that is not so big you will never do it); Relevant (the goal should make sense for your situation); Time-bound (something that you can do in a day or a week, so that the task is not long-drawn-out).

DAY 2
WHAT WOULD JESUS DO?

Q. 20: To what extent does your reading of the Bible point you towards Jesus and how to live for him?

Jesus went throughout Galilee, teaching in their syna-
gogues, proclaiming the good news of the kingdom, and
healing every disease and sickness among the people. News
about him spread all over Syria, and people brought to
him all who were ill with various diseases, those suffering
severe pain, the demon-possessed, those having seizures,
and the paralysed; and he healed them. Large crowds from
Galilee, the Decapolis, Jerusalem, Judea and the region
across the Jordan followed him.
(Matthew 4.23–25)

As followers of Jesus, we recognize that Jesus is our template for life. Even so, our lives often look very similar to
the ones of those who don't know him. The model we see
in the Bible is that of apprenticeship. The disciples wanted
to learn and to grow to be like Jesus in character. They
always watched him very closely and did what he did.
They would then try these things for themselves and come
back to reflect with Jesus on what happened. This is and
was the training model of the rabbis (Jewish teachers)
during the time of Jesus. Today, we should want to do the
same: as we read about the life of Jesus in the Gospels, we

should allow what we see to shape us. Jesus is the template and our goal is to become more like him.

Jesus' day had a several parts (if you remove eating, sleeping, laughing and so on).

1 Proclaiming the kingdom of God (or the presence of God).
2 Teaching and helping others in the way of God.
3 Praying for and healing the sick.
4 Praying for the possessed and casting out demons.
5 Retreating, fasting and praying.
6 Prophesying and being prophetic (giving attention to hearing what God wanted to do).
7 Fighting and challenging social injustice.
8 Eating and drinking with those seen as unpopular.
9 Challenging religious people and power.
10 Speaking truth to power.

In his day, Jesus had a clear ministry and teaching role that many of us do not have. We are not necessarily expected to live our lives as rabbis and touring evangelists, as Jesus did. We might be teachers, students, police officers, office workers, builders or musicians; the challenge is to allow Jesus' example to start to permeate our day. Some of Jesus' actions, such as casting out demons, we are unlikely to do because we are not going to encounter that sort of situation often, if at all. However, there are activities that Jesus did that can be part of our daily lives, such as praying for people to be free from the things that trap them.

YES, BUT HOW?
Look at the table overleaf. How many of the activities listed in the chart do you recognize in your own life? How

What Jesus did	Never	Sometimes	All the time
Proclaiming the kingdom of God			
Teaching and helping others in the way of God			
Praying for and healing the sick			
Praying for the possessed and casting out demons			
Retreating, fasting and praying			
Prophesying and being prophetic (giving attention to hearing what God wants to do)			
Fighting and challenging social injustice			
Eating and drinking with those seen as unpopular			
Challenging religious people and power			
Speaking truth to power			
Total			

many of them do you do all the time and how many rarely occur? You might like to look at the chart again and tot up how many you do. We have to acknowledge that our days are very different from those of Jesus – many of us have to drop the kids at school, do the weekly shop, go to university and so on. Nevertheless, the challenge remains: how can those activities that we 'never' do become ones we 'sometimes' do? How can those we 'sometimes' do become ones we do 'all the time'?

QUESTIONS TO CONSIDER

- Is there someone who inspires you and might be able to coach you in starting to live more like Jesus?
- Do you have someone around you to whom you could draw closer, with the aim of seeing how he or she lives out faith in Jesus?
- If you are exploring Christianity or are new to it, perhaps you could visit a local church to start to get to know other followers of Jesus.

PRAYER

Father,
your son spoke of the kingdom so powerfully.
Please help us by anointing our lips to do the same in our own way.
Give us the confidence and courage to speak words of life over and around people.
Please help us to see those who are open and ready for your kingdom.
Amen.

DAY 3
RETREAT TO ADVANCE

Q. 9: How engaged are you in a personal and community prayer life?

After he had dismissed them, he went up on a mountainside by himself to pray. Later that night, he was there alone, and the boat was already a considerable distance from land, buffeted by the waves because the wind was against it.

Shortly before dawn Jesus went out to them, walking on the lake. When the disciples saw him walking on the lake, they were terrified. 'It's a ghost,' they said, and cried out in fear.

But Jesus immediately said to them: 'Take courage! It is I. Don't be afraid.'
(Matthew 14.23–27)

Modern life feels as if it's just getting faster, with more to do. Technology that promised to make life easier and give us more time has simply allowed us to cram extra stuff into our days, making us busier than ever. We are more productive and yet more disconnected than we have ever been. It appears that what was meant to be our servant has become our master. People are working longer hours and spending less time with their families.

At the same time, we each have concerns which we long to see breakthroughs for. For some, the desire is for improved finances; for others, it's for improved health or for a more satisfactory family life or marriage. We each have aspects of our lives that we desperately want to change, but our prayers don't always bring the results we want.

Much of the time, Jesus was surrounded not only by crowds of people but also by impossible tasks or problems. In today's passage, we see that he did something that regularly occurs in the Gospels – before he performed many of his miracles, he retreated to hills, mountains or high ground to pray.

Jesus retreated to advance.

Before Jesus advanced through a problem, such as healing a girl, feeding 5,000 people or, as in today's reading, walking on water, he always hit pause. He retreated to a quiet place to pray so that he could meet the challenge. Sometimes, the Gospels indicate that Jesus fasted as well as prayed, and that was why he was able to experience breakthroughs.

There is a danger that sometimes we want the breakthrough without doing what Jesus did and said. Jesus teaches us that we should *'go into [our] room*, close the door and pray to [our] Father, who is unseen. Then [our] Father, who sees what is done in secret, will reward [us]' (Matthew 6.6). Jesus' 'room' was a mountain or hill; he tells us to find a quiet spot – whether a room, a wide, open field or a mountain – and to enter into a place of prayer. In doing so, God will engage with us.

A while ago, a friend and I were walking on the Thames Path, near the Thames Barrier, when we realized we were lost. It was getting dark and we didn't know how we had strayed off the clearly demarcated way. We were struggling and needed help. We decided to hit pause; we stopped walking and took some time to focus, to work out where we were and to find someone to help us get back on track. We received some help from an old man who walked past, found where we were on the map and then continued on the right path.

Perhaps we are more lost than we would like to admit and that we need to hit pause more often to get back on track.

YES, BUT HOW?

Make some space to retreat. A retreat can happen at a retreat centre, where the staff can help you to take time to slow down. You can create your own retreat by going for a long walk or by hiding in a safe place at home – going into a room and shutting the door. Creating a retreat doesn't take much; it's simply about making time to hit pause.

1 **Find a place to stop**, whether it is a comfy chair or an open field. Either way, find a spot where you can shut out all the tasks at hand and allow yourself to breathe.
2 **Watch your breathing**, become aware of your own body and any tension it is carrying. While doing so, simply pray, 'Father, come and find me.' Allow yourself time to become aware of God's presence and enjoy the quiet.
3 **P.R.A.Y.** (see right): if you find it helpful, use this acronym to structure your time. Your prayers don't have to be clever, long and complex. Say it as it is. Be normal.

A SIMPLE WAY TO

P. PAUSE
Life never seems to take a breath. Every day there is something to deal with. Take a moment to pause and say 'hello' to Jesus. Breathe deeply and focus on how your body feels. Allow yourself to relax and become aware of God's presence.

R. REJOICE
God is always at work. Take some time to rejoice and be thankful for what God has done for you and those you love. Rejoice in Jesus and his death for you. Tell God how grateful you are for him and all that he has done. Specifically name the things that you appreciate from the day or week. Having a grateful heart is about having a 'great full heart'.

A. ASK
Once you have been grateful, take time to tell God how you are. What do you need at present? Pray for issues that affect you and your loved ones. Take time to pray for . . . wisdom, peace, breakthroughs in political issues, global issues, community groups and so on and so on. Nothing is off the table or too small or big. Simply use your own words to tell God what's going on.

Y. YIELD
Yielding is simply about saying 'yes' to Jesus. God knows best and knows what the best response is to your prayers. Tell God that you are willing to yield to his work and wisdom. Yielding is about recognizing that he is king and we are his servants.

AMEN. This means 'so be it'. We say 'so be it' to mean God is in control. He knows best and we agree to the prayer prayed. It can be expressed in endless ways, from a soft whisper to a joyous shout.

DAY 4
DO YOU LOVE THE KINDS OF PEOPLE JESUS LOVED?

Q. 13: To what extent is your heart in line with God's love and desire?

Love the Lord your God with all your heart and with all your soul and with all your strength and with all your mind'; and, 'Love your neighbour as yourself'.
(Luke 10.27)

Jesus was a beautiful storyteller. He had material that he composed himself but he also had a gift for putting a fresh twist on old tales.

In Jesus' time, there was a story told about a man travelling the narrow road running from Jericho to Jerusalem. It's worth searching on the Internet for some images of this iconic road to see what it looks like. If you do take a look, you will see that it twists and turns at many points. It is so narrow that if someone were travelling the road with a wide load, it would be hard to pass by them without falling off the edge. In the story, the man is attacked by bandits, beaten and left for dead. Being left for dead is an important thing to note: in the first century, a Jewish spiritual leader had to avoid touching dead things to make sure that he was ceremonially clean for his priestly or pastoral ministry. Contact with a dead body would compromise this role, making him unable to fulfil his priestly duties.

Three people pass by the man who has been left for dead on this narrow road. The first is a priest who, on seeing the man, believes he is dead. He steps around him and walks on to ensure that he remains ritually pure, able to fulfil his duties as a priest. The second person to walk by is a Levite who serves at the temple and also has to remain pure to assist the priest. In the original story, the third person that comes upon the man is a Jewish layman, who is heading to Jerusalem to worship and probably offer a sacrifice. The Jewish layman helps the man in the road and takes him to a nearby guest house.

The function of this original story was to remind Jewish people about knowing their place in a religiously tiered society. Priests and Levites had their roles in the temple but ordinary Jews had their place too. Their roles involved tasks that the priests and Levites could not readily do, such as showing love to the poor, the abandoned or the needy.

Jesus took this story and added a new perspective or, as I like to think of it, a 'Jesus twist'. In Jesus' version, the first two characters that walk by are the same – a priest and a Levite. However, Jesus takes the third character, the Jewish layman, and turns him into a Samaritan. It is hard for us to imagine the contempt that first-century Jews had for Samaritans. The Samaritans were deeply hated for ethnic and religious reasons. They were seen as an impure race with a faulty understanding of the Jewish God. So Jesus retells a story about knowing one's place in society and turns it into a mirror that reflects and exposes the listeners' own prejudice and hatred for other human beings. Jesus' first-century audience would have been astonished and angered by his version of the story.

Even so, Jesus doesn't change the story just to point out human prejudice. He does so to make one radical point: that he loves the Samaritans as much as the Jews. Until the Jews understood that Jesus was for all people, they would miss out on the beautiful, wider perspective of God in the world. God revealed through Jesus that he loved everyone: Jew and Samaritan; Jew and Gentile. There is no one outside the Jewish people that God does not love.

If I asked you to mark out of 10 how loving you were, with 10 for being totally loving and 1 for being totally unloving, I wonder how you would mark yourself? Are we as loving as we think we are and do we love like Jesus loved? Loving someone in the way Jesus loved is much more than being kind to the other person.

1 Jesus' love was a **costly** love (John 13.15, 31–32).
2 Jesus' love was a **caring** love (John 13.33).
3 Jesus' love was a deeply **committed** love (John 13.34).

John 13.34 reads, 'A new commandment I give to you, that you love one another: just as I have loved you, you are also to love one another' (ESV). The key here is 'as I have loved you'. Can we love with the depth that Jesus loved to the point of full sacrifice?

YES, BUT HOW?

Imagine Jesus telling you the story about the battered man on the Jericho road today. Who would he have as the third character? Who is your 'Samaritan'? Which kind of person would Jesus put in the story to challenge you? You will only know who if you are completely honest. For some of us, it might be a member of the Taliban; for others, a homeless heroin addict, a transgender person or simply a noisy neighbour.

Who is your 'Samaritan'? _____

Those you dislike or are prejudiced against are loved by God. God will never advocate your dislike of another person. Growing to appreciate someone you really struggle with is a hard journey and one that takes time, but it always starts with our praying for God's forgiveness and help. Take a moment to confess your struggles with an individual or group of people and then ask for forgiveness.

PRAYER

Father,

forgive me for my anger and hatred towards _____.

Please forgive me and lead me to see them the way you see them.

Help me to grow to love them just as you do.

Amen.

DAY 5
A LULLABY FOR WAR

Q. 9: How engaged are you in a personal and community prayer life?

> Whoever dwells in the shelter of the Most High
>   will rest in the shadow of the Almighty.
> I will say of the LORD, 'He is my refuge and my fortress,
>   my God, in whom I trust.'
>
> Surely he will save you
>   from the fowler's snare
>   and from the deadly pestilence.
> He will cover you with his feathers,
>   and under his wings you will find refuge;
>   his faithfulness will be your shield and rampart.
> (Psalm 91.1–4)

Picture a full-blown battle raging all around you. Shots being fired, missiles flying, aircraft roaring. You are dodging bullets and fending off attacks and barrages of assault. Then you stop. Desperate, you reach into your rucksack and pull out . . .

[*pause*]

What are you fighting? What's your personal war? It could be stress at work or strife in your family, mental ill-health, physical pain or old wounds. But, ultimately, the

Bible suggests that there is a dark evil behind these things that distort and hurt us. Psalm 91 gives this opposing force many names but the Church, through the ages, has simply called him 'the enemy'. We know that Jesus' love on the cross was victorious (Romans 8.35–39) and that there will be a day when the enemy is fully defeated and when Jesus will wipe away every tear (Revelation 21.4) but, for now, there is still war.

[*un-pause*]

. . . you reach into your rucksack and pull out a plastic mobile, the kind that you would hang over a baby's cot. You hold it up: its colours are vivid against your dirty skin and the smokey air. You tug the string, a lullaby begins to play, somehow overcoming the sounds of war. You smile, curl up and fall fast asleep.

Psalm 91 is a lullaby for God's army. It is a promise of protection in the midst of what it might seem impossible to survive; it invites us into a new way of existing in the fight – through rest. No matter what is going on around us, we can rest in God, like a young bird nestling under its mother's wing. Here, we discover the best armour there is (Ephesians 6.10–17).

Reflect on Jesus for a moment. In Matthew 8.23–27, we are told that when a storm hit the boat, the disciples were in panic mode, worrying about the boat tipping over and, all the while, Jesus was resting. There was an obvious peace within Jesus that is hard to understand on occasion. How could Jesus be so peaceful when things were going wrong? Jesus was sleeping through the storm because he knew the bigger picture and trusted in his father.

Jesus knew the reality of Exodus 14.14: 'The LORD will fight for you; you need only to be still.' Sometimes the battle is not fought with panic, by going faster or doing more. Sometimes the battle is won by resting, pausing and anchoring ourselves to the Father, who will lift us up and fight for us, if only we would remain still.

YES, BUT HOW?

On different pieces of paper, write down those problems that you are battling against. Add the struggles being faced by your church, neighbourhood, country or the world. Somewhere private, arrange the pieces on the floor, with space in the middle of them. Read through Psalm 91 below, giving the issues on the paper to God and declaring your trust in him.

Read through Psalm 91 again. Highlight the key phrases that speak to you and bring encouragement to you today.

PSALM 91

Whoever dwells in the shelter of the Most High
    will rest in the shadow of the Almighty.
I will say of the LORD, 'He is my refuge and my
     fortress,
    my God, in whom I trust.'

Surely he will save you
    from the fowler's snare
    and from the deadly pestilence.
He will cover you with his feathers,
    and under his wings you will find refuge;
    his faithfulness will be your shield and
     rampart.
You will not fear the terror of night,
    nor the arrow that flies by day,

A LULLABY FOR WAR

nor the pestilence that stalks in the darkness,
    nor the plague that destroys at midday.
A thousand may fall at your side,
    ten thousand at your right hand,
    but it will not come near you.
You will only observe with your eyes
    and see the punishment of the wicked.

If you say, 'The LORD is my refuge,'
    and you make the Most High your dwelling,
no harm will overtake you,
    no disaster will come near your tent.
For he will command his angels concerning you
    to guard you in all your ways;
they will lift you up in their hands,
    so that you will not strike your foot against a
        stone.
You will tread on the lion and the cobra;
    you will trample the great lion and the serpent.

'Because he loves me,' says the LORD, 'I will rescue
        him;
    I will protect him, for he acknowledges my
        name.
He will call on me, and I will answer him;
    I will be with him in trouble,
    I will deliver him and honour him.
With long life I will satisfy him
    and show him my salvation.'

DAY 6
WOULD ANYONE NOTICE IF YOU WEREN'T A CHRISTIAN?

Q. 11: To what extent are areas of sin and brokenness in your life being changed by Jesus?

You are the salt of the earth. But if the salt loses its saltiness, how can it be made salty again? It is no longer good for anything, except to be thrown out and trampled underfoot. You are the light of the world. A town built on a hill cannot be hidden.
(Matthew 5.13–16)

What identifies you as a Christian?
Socks and sandals? *Check.*
Quiche for the bring and share? *Check.*

It looks as if you're all ready to go out into the world and be identified as a follower of Jesus. OK, so that's not how it works. It's all about the reusable coffee cup, the beard that's just the right length (sorry, ladies) and the ability to sing 'Amazing Grace' in your sleep. Again, I joke. I start with some easy laughs because, if I'm honest, the question bothers me more than I want to admit. Would anyone notice if I weren't a Christian? Would they, though? What makes my faith so life changing that someone would notice if it weren't there next week?

Many years ago, a friend of mine stood up to tell her testimony. She was a woman who was so desperate to fit in that she did everything she could to dance between being a Christian and not being noticed as a Christian. She would go out to parties with friends at the weekend. Occasionally, she'd drink a little too much and have the odd cigarette. One day, as she was sitting with her friend having lunch on a park bench, her friend said, 'What I love about you is that you're not like those other Christians. You are exactly like us.' My friend realized that what, at first glance, appeared to be a compliment actually wasn't. Initially, she thought her friend was saying 'You are just like me and you have a faith', but what her friend was actually saying was 'You're just like me and I don't see your faith'.

How do your work colleagues, neighbours and friends see you and your faith? Is it a beautiful aspect of your life or is it almost non-existent?

It's a very challenging question but one we must wrestle with. Jesus says that we are salt, but have we lost our saltiness? Jesus makes it clear: if we have lost the distinct nature of being one of his followers, then we are nothing but something to be 'trampled underfoot'.

In Jesus' day, salt was used as an antiseptic and a preservative; it was used to preserve food, to clean and to help human waste to decompose. It was also used for flavour in cooking. Like salt, we are to be a holy antiseptic and something that brings out a 'God flavour'.

I challenge you to find five minutes today to sit quietly and ask yourself whether your faith is visible or not. Then sit in silence and see what comes to mind.

Can you write down what would look different about your day to anyone else, if you were not a Christian?

THANK GOD

Spend some time thanking God for the things that are already different, for the ways he has changed your life on this journey that we are taking together.

ASK GOD

Spend some time asking God to help you with those things that you wish looked different, that you know have no place in the life of someone following the one who set you free. It might be something that you do or an attitude that you have. It might be an easy thing to start to change or it might be something that is going to take a lifetime of journeying with Jesus.

PRAYER

Father God,

Creator of the universe, I approach you with a grateful heart for all that you have given me.

I submit all that I am to you, and give you the honour and praise that are due to you.

I was created in your image –

fearfully and wonderfully made to be the salt and light in this dark world.

Guide me in a path of righteousness, according to your will and glory.

Shape me and form me into the likeness of Jesus, and help me to behave like him today.

Amen.

DAY 7
WASHED CLEAN

Q. 11: To what extent are areas of sin and brokenness in your life being changed by Jesus?

> Have mercy on me, O God,
>   according to your unfailing love;
> according to your great compassion
>   blot out my transgressions.
> Wash away all my iniquity
>   and cleanse me from my sin.
>
> For I know my transgressions
>   and my sin is always before me.
> (Psalm 51.1–3)

As part of my ministry, I sit with people, young and old, to talk about the grace of Jesus. I sat with one gentleman who was coming to faith later in life. Before one service, he started to tell me a few things he had done over the years. I sensed that there was more to come, so we booked a time to meet. He went on to tell me everything that he had done in his life, and how not telling anyone about it was eating him alive. He hadn't murdered anyone, but there were little things he had done at work to force someone out so that he could rise up the ranks; lies that he had told in past relationships to cover his tracks; and broken relationships with his children because he didn't want to give them his time. All these things had mounted up and he was crippled by them. After years of living like this, he came to realize that he was now dwelling in a prison that he himself had made. Until we confess our sin, we are locked in prison cells of our own making. We end up being trapped by the effects of the sin, the lies we tell to cover up our sin and the guilt that comes to consume us.

The story goes that there was once a man with great faith in God. During a flood, he was in danger of drowning, so climbed on to the roof of his house. After some time, a fisherman in a boat approached and invited him to jump aboard. The man quickly responded, 'Thank you but I don't need your help; I trust God alone.' The fisherman left and the water rose. A short time later, a helicopter passed by. The helicopter pilot hung out of the window and offered to help the man. Once again, he rejected the help, saying that he would trust God alone. Later that day, the man drowned and went to heaven.

He looked at God and said, 'God, I am so disappointed with you. I trusted you with all my heart and look what happened to me!'

God responded, 'My son, I too am disappointed; I sent you a fisherman and a helicopter, what are you doing here?!'

Sometimes supernatural help looks natural. It's just how God works. Remember Genesis 22 when Abraham is about to sacrifice Isaac? To prevent the death of Isaac, God provides a ram in a thicket. God works in natural ways by supernatural means.

I would describe myself as a recovering porn addict who has found freedom. Even so, I'm aware that I have to make a daily choice. When it was a real problem, a friend of mine suggested that I install a porn blocker on all my electronic devices, to stop me using them when the thought popped into my mind. I remember my response: 'I don't need this, bro. I have God in my life.' In my arrogance, I was telling somebody who had found freedom from the obsession that I didn't need his help, even though I was the one watching porn. I carried on praying, expecting God to take the desire away, but the situation just deteriorated. I started to watch even more and to feel worse and worse.

Sometimes, we expect God to do everything for us without any personal effort. I wanted to be free but when God sent the 'fisherman' I said, 'No thanks.' It was only when I surrendered, went to the fisherman and asked for help that God eventually lifted the obsession. God will wash away our iniquities but we have a part to play.

When we confess to someone else, we start to allow the light to come into the dark corners. When we confess and allow ourselves to surrender to the will of God, then we can start to see lasting change.

YES, BUT HOW?

Think of an area of your life that you would like God to cleanse.

What is the soap that you might need to buy?

What can you put in place today to stop yourself giving into bad habits and ways of life?

Hold out your hands in front of you. Imagine that your bad attitudes and behaviours are in your hands. Which of them don't you like?

Which of your behaviours does God want you to get rid of?

Imagine washing your hands and giving these attitudes and behaviours to God. Confess and ask God to make you holy according to his love.

Have mercy on me, O God,
   according to your unfailing love;
according to your great compassion
   blot out my transgressions.
Wash away all my iniquity
   and cleanse me from my sin.

For I know my transgressions,
   and my sin is always before me.
(Psalm 51.1–3)

DAY 8
SOUL FOOD

Q. 17: How much time do you regularly spend engaging with the Bible?

> As the deer pants for streams of water,
>   so my soul pants for you, my God.
> My soul thirsts for God, for the living God.
>   When can I go and meet with God?
> (Psalm 42.1–2)

Have you ever been on a long hike and run out of water? It might be that you went out for the day and realized that you didn't bring a drink with you. Have you ever been out-side on a hot summer's day and not had enough to drink and you started to feel sick, dizzy or strange?

We notice our physical thirst for water much more quickly than we notice our souls thirsting for God. It's easy to feel that we haven't drunk enough, but harder at times to see when we haven't connected with God enough. The more you understand your spiritual needs, the more you will notice when they are not met. That's why David links spiritual thirst with a deer panting in the Judean heat. When we thirst for God, we can either go to the stream of living water or try to drink from the quick fix that is TV, shopping, a bottle of wine, family, friends or porno-graphy. These are things we can drink in the hope that they will quench our thirst and make us feel contented and refreshed.

God has everything we need and has given us ways to access his provision every day. Daily prayer, reading the Bible and encountering the Holy Spirit are the three things we need to feed our souls. Doing the 3-2-1 daily retreat (see page 12) is the best place to start. Today, let's focus on the Bible and how to get everything we need from it.

Have you ever read a Bible passage and found that it didn't make sense to you? The answer may often be 'yes'. Why is it so hard to understand the Bible? Doesn't God want us to know what he's saying? Is he a complicated God?

The Bible is sometimes hard for us to grasp because it is a collection of different books, written for different occasions for people in completely different times and contexts! But this is the good news: we don't need to understand everything! It is completely normal for a passage to make little sense to us. Why? The purpose of reading the Bible is not to understand it perfectly, to gain great knowledge; it is the place where we encounter God.

Do you have any habits that feel as necessary to you as eating food and drinking water? Perhaps they might include listening to music while taking a shower, having a cup of tea in the morning, reading the newspaper, having a Twix after lunch or looking at your favourite app.

Imagine if *reading the Bible* became an essential habit. It may be difficult if we read the Bible simply to gain knowledge. But if reading the Bible speaks into our everyday lives, touches our hearts and makes our souls feel at home with God, it becomes a worthwhile daily experience. God wants to nourish our spirits and speak into our personal lives, struggles, thoughts and feelings through the Bible.

Let's start reading the Bible and experience doing so as a life-giving habit!

YES, BUT HOW?

HOW TO READ THE BIBLE

We need God to speak to us, to both our minds and our hearts. If we are left to our own devices, the world and culture around us will shape us, not God. Here, we spend some time letting God shape us, using an old Bible-reading practice called the Swedish Bible study method, described below. This shaping of our minds can happen when we engage with the Holy Spirit through the Bible. Start by taking

WHAT JUMPS OUT AT ME?

This should be something in the passage that grabs your attention; something challenging, inspiring or weird.

ANY BURNING QUESTIONS?

This is anything that you find hard to understand or you wish you could ask the writer. There's no question too silly.

WHAT ABOUT GOD?

God is not made up from our imagination. He is real and made us to be friends with him. What does this show about his nature and intentions?

WHAT ABOUT PEOPLE?

We are made in his image but that image has been distorted by ego, fear and pain. What does this reveal about who we were made to be?

WHAT AM I GOING TO DO?

We are invited by Jesus to live life to the full. We learn by doing. What are you going to do about what you've read?

the Gospel of Matthew (or another Gospel). As you read or listen to a short section of the Bible, take a moment to pray that God will speak to you through it, then use the questions shown in the illustration on the previous page to help you to hear him.

As you read, take note of and focus on what stands out for you – it might be that God is speaking to you. You may not always get 'light-bulb' moments but, if you persevere, you can be sure that there will be some.

There are devotional books that help to link Bible passages to everyday life. Speak to Christians you know to see whether they have any recommendations. You may also find it helpful to share with others what you've experienced when reading the Bible.

DAY 9
YOUR DESIRES OR GOD'S DESIRES?

Q. 13: To what extent is your heart in line with God's love and desire?

After removing Saul, he made David their king. God testified concerning him: 'I have found David son of Jesse, a man after my own heart; he will do everything I want him to do.'
(Acts 13.22)

When a thousand voices in our culture tell you to follow your heart, beware. Because, as Jeremiah 17.9 tells us, 'The heart is deceitful above all things, and desperately sick; who can understand it?' (ESV).

Very sadly, a few months ago one of my very close friends died from a heart attack. He didn't seem especially unwell and none of us realized that there were any problems with his heart. Why would we? We couldn't see inside him. It wasn't until he had passed away that the doctors realized all his arteries were blocked. There can be so many issues with our bodies that we don't know are there until it is too late. An early diagnosis is key to survival. It is similar when it comes to our spiritual illnesses.

We can be spiritually sick and able to hide it, or not even know it, until it's too late. Saul, the first king of Israel, had become spiritually sick. He was sick with pride, arrogance, power and a lust for empire. We often see this in the Bible, when people enter roles with humility and then fall from grace because they become sick with power and their hearts become unwell.

In the Bible, the 'heart' usually means the place where emotions, thoughts and intentions come from. It's the heart that shows what a person is really like.

In today's verse it says that God removed Saul, who was the king before David. His heart had become self-centred, arrogant and jealous. He had stopped listening to what God was saying or caring about God's concerns. He became focused only on his own interests. Saul's heart-sickness stopped him from being the godly king needed for Israel, so David was made king instead because he was in sympathy with the heart of God. David had the same priorities and values that God had, and pleasing God was his main motivation.

If we trace the whole story of David, from shepherd boy to king, we see that he was far from perfect and made some very serious mistakes. In fact, like Saul, sickness started to creep into his heart but, unlike Saul, David made changes. Psalm 51 was written by him after he did something that was very wrong. In the psalm, he asked God to give him a clean heart; the good news was that God was willing to do this for David, just as he is for us.

There is a delusionary power to sin – so much so that when it grips the human heart, it can make ordinarily sane and reasonable people do completely outrageous things. I've often met amazing people who made stupid decisions that ruined their lives. I once read about a woman who worked as a tailor for a prison in New York. She was found guilty of helping two convicted killers escape by smuggling hacksaw blades and screwdrivers to them in frozen hamburgers. When asked why, it turned out that she had developed a romantic and physical relationship with both convicts. She said they made her feel special and they had planned to kill her husband on their release. We have to ask how a mature woman's heart could be turned in this way by such foolish wickedness.

God sees our hearts even when they are invisible to everyone else. We come to know his heart as we read the Bible, listen to other followers of Jesus and ask God to show us how our hearts need to be changed.

YES, BUT HOW?

Look at the heart below. Within it there are some sicknesses we can have. Which of them do you recognize as yours? Which sicknesses would you add?

PRIDE   ANGER
IMMORALITY   MURDER
LUST
FRAUD   WASTEFULNESS
FOOLISHNESS   GUILT
DECEIT   RECKLESSNESS
GLUTTONY   HATE
COVERTNESS
LIES

Let us draw near to God with a sincere heart and with the full assurance that faith brings, having our hearts sprinkled to cleanse us from a guilty conscience and having our bodies washed with pure water.
(Hebrews 10.22)

Over the next few days, take special note of how your words, attitudes and actions demonstrate the state of your heart – the source of it all – and ask God to work in you, cleaning you up, healing you and helping you to have a heart like his.

PRAYER

Jesus,
I draw near with an honest heart,
    committed to you and full of trust in your good news.
Cleanse my heart and make it clean;
    remove from me the guilt and shame for what I have done.
This day, please help me to align my heart with yours,
    and break my heart for what breaks yours.
Amen.

DAY 10
WHAT IS SO IMPORTANT ABOUT CHURCH?

Q. 2: How committed are you to a local church community?

After they prayed, the place where they were meeting was shaken. And they were all filled with the Holy Spirit and spoke the word of God boldly. All the believers were one in heart and mind.
(Acts 4.31–32)

I often hear this statement: 'I don't need to go to church to be a Christian.' What is so important about the Church? There are so many answers to this question. Here are some examples.

- The local church is God's place for us to be discipled and make disciples.
- The local church is the place to find fellowship. We are told by psychologists that we are basically a composite of the five people with whom we spend the most time. Church is a place to keep our faith on fire with others.
- The voice of a good Bible-teaching church helps to counteract the deception that surrounds us during the week.
- Weekly ministry and service in a local church helps us to build our spiritual muscles.

- The Church counteracts the materialistic, consumer attitude and the sinful 'me-centered' world view.
- The Church is a family of people on a mission together. It is not a place for individuals to consume but where each of us play our part in its common life.

There was once an old rabbi of deep faith who was sat beside a coal fire on a winter's night with his young disciple.

'Rabbi, why must we attend synagogue when the people are just so ghastly, the music is not to my taste and the hospitality is so poor?' asked the young man.

The Rabbi didn't speak but simply grasped some fire tongs. Picking up a red-hot coal, he placed it on the hearth. During the next few minutes, the coal went from white to yellow, to red and then to black. Eventually the Rabbi picked up the now cold coal with his own hands and threw it back into the fire. 'That is why,' he said.

Today's verses from Acts point to one answer in particular. When the believers joined together as a people, as a family, and cried out to God as one in prayer, the Holy Spirit was poured out on them. They were united by the Spirit, and equipped to go out boldly and share the gospel with confidence.

We can certainly serve God as individuals. The hermit living alone in the mountains isn't invisible or useless to God. Personal prayer and communing with the Father alone are huge parts of building our relationship with him. But what these verses tell us is that when we, as followers of Jesus, come together in relationship in the family called church, God moves among us, joins us as a family on a mission for him, and gives us the tools to go out to serve him and make disciples.

In Matthew 18.20, Jesus says, 'For where two or three gather in my name, there am I with them.' When we go to church on a Sunday, meet in small groups mid-week, help at missions and do ministry, work with children and young people, help at night shelters and food banks, when we share the same space, praying together, worshipping, learning and serving together, the Bible says that God meets with us by his Spirit. When we meet together as a family, we give God the space to meet with us powerfully.

We give God the opportunity to unite us in our differences. He doesn't want to make us all the same in every way; he wants us to be on the same page, with one mission, and to be filled with the same spirit and passion. We allow God to equip us with exactly what we need to go out into our individual, day-to-day mission-orientated fields when we come together as the Church. The gathered Church allows our Father to bring us together as a family, meet with us powerfully, and equip us to be a sent church, living out his kingdom in the world.

We **connect** to one another and to Jesus; we then **grow** in knowledge, character and action. From this, we go to **serve**, using our personal attributes for Jesus' mission, which enables us to **share** Jesus and the good news with others.

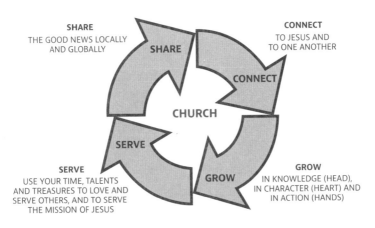

SHARE
THE GOOD NEWS LOCALLY AND GLOBALLY

CONNECT
TO JESUS AND TO ONE ANOTHER

CHURCH

SERVE
USE YOUR TIME, TALENTS AND TREASURES TO LOVE AND SERVE OTHERS, AND TO SERVE THE MISSION OF JESUS

GROW
IN KNOWLEDGE (HEAD), IN CHARACTER (HEART) AND IN ACTION (HANDS)

YES, BUT HOW?

QUESTIONS TO CONSIDER

- How often do you attend a Sunday church service?
- Are you committed to a small group or midweek discipleship group?
- Have you ever left a church because you found something you didn't like? Has this happened repeatedly or only once?
- If you have left a number of churches because of a problem, you may well have had a bad run, but it is also worth asking: do I have too high an expectation? Do I find it hard to live in harmony with others? Could I have done anything differently?
- How involved are you with church? Do you think it's important in your week and life?
- Do you need to make a greater commitment to being part of a church community and playing your part?

YOUR BROTHER HAS BEEN BEATEN

Q. 18: To what extent are you regularly discovering more about Jesus and his work in our world?

Remember the word that I said to you: 'A servant is not greater than his master.' If they persecuted me, they will also persecute you. If they kept my word, they will also keep yours.
(John 15.20 ESV)

Did you know that there are 2.4 billion Christians in the world? Did you also know that a hundred million Christians experience high, very high or extreme persecution?

We can live our lives in a little bubble in which we see our faith as part of our world and life. But if we were to step back to see what was happening to our global family, we would be shocked. Imagine not being able to go to church in daylight. Imagine not being able to sing in church for fear of being heard. Imagine having to hide your Bible at home so that it can't be found in a search. Imagine that, for the safety of your family, you denounce your faith. Imagine not even telling your family. Imagine being imprisoned for your faith.

In 2018, I spent some time in Lebanon, visiting a Syrian church that had relocated because of persecution and war. I was amazed by the passion I found in these persecuted members of my Christian family. One Syrian pastor said to me:

> You forget how beautiful the light is until you're forced into the dark. For many Christians, the darkness has given them a great vision of the light of Jesus. The war was a gift; it made us wake up to the reality that humanity is lost without Jesus. I've seen many survive persecution but not many survive prosperity. Sadly, in the West you're more in love with life than you are with Jesus, and it makes you unwilling to die for him. The little daily distractions around you are killing your faith. You're distracted by the mundane and you miss the light all around you.

How true are his comments? It might be worth rereading what he said a few times. There was so much in what he said that stood out for me, but none more than '*I've seen many survive persecution but not many survive prosperity*'.

There is a danger that we are sleeping Christians. Unaware of the reality around us, drugged on our prosperity and blinded by our security. Sitting with this group of homeless brothers and sisters made me realize how easy we have it, and how we disrespect them each day by being lukewarm for our faith.

Jesus specifically called the Christian family a 'body'; this wasn't just a nice sermon illustration – it described the reality of the whole family of God. The blood of Jesus unifies us all, so when one of us bleeds, we should all be aware of the pain. If we are to be the genuine family of God, then we should be aware of when our body is hurting.

Let's truly appreciate the freedom that we have to practise our faith. Let's not miss the work of Jesus around us.

Let's pray for persecuted Christians but let's also be in-spired by them as people dedicated to the Way of Jesus.

YES, BUT HOW?

Take time today to pray for the Christians in the top ten most persecuted countries. Pray that they will remain strong and steadfast in the face of persecution. Pray, 'Lord be real to them, give them what they need, and may they know your presence.'

1 North Korea
2 Afghanistan
3 Somalia
4 Libya
5 Pakistan
6 Sudan
7 Eritrea
8 Yemen
9 Iran
10 India

PRAYER

God, you know the plight of people far away.
Oppressed by governments and vigilantes in places
    where Christianity is an unpopular choice.
God, you knew
that the day would come here when truth-telling
    would be despised and siding with the
    oppressed part of the road less travelled.
Have mercy, O God,
upon persecuted Christians, there and here,
who are willing to suffer the consequences
for speaking your name
in word or in deed,
in defiance or in advocacy.
Grant courage and strength
to all who would dare
to live their convictions out loud.
Amen.
(Safiyah Fosua, 'A prayer for persecuted Christians',
based on Luke 21.12, written for the International
Day of Prayer for Persecuted Christians)

DAY 12
THE PLACE WHERE WE ARE

Q.19: How often do you regularly discuss your faith with others?

Whenever you are arrested and brought to trial, do not worry beforehand about what to say. Just say whatever is given you at the time, for it is not you speaking, but the Holy Spirit.
(Mark 13.11)

Our lives can often seem mundane, boring and ordinary. At times, it even seems as if our lives are just coincidences, that we just happen to be here.

The truth, though, is that we all have a call from God – to be those who share God's story, God's hope and God's love in all the places we find ourselves. Our stories are not just coincidences, they can be used by God's Spirit, living in us, to inspire change and transformation.

The story of the early Church was one of persecution. Christians were dragged into court for saying that they were Jesus' followers, their lives determined not by a 'call' but by their chains. And yet, in that place, they knew what to say and how to behave because the Spirit was with them. In his letters, Paul says that he saw being in prison as a great opportunity because it allowed him to share Jesus with those around him (Philippians 1.12–14).

A friend of mine works in a school as a head of department. It's a normal school job with normal children, yet he found a place to live out his faith:

As a maths teacher, I felt as if I had no time even to think about God, let alone share my faith. I was rushing from lesson to lesson, to meetings, to marking, to preparation, to crashing out with tiredness at home. But I knew God had me there for a reason and, looking back, I see how the Holy Spirit was at work, guiding and using me in those places. I gave a witness to colleagues through the way I behaved with grace and integrity, in conversations about faith with some of my Muslim students, and in having the courage to start a lunchtime discussion group about Jesus with any students who wanted to come. I now see how my faith shaped and had an impact on how I was in school. School wasn't normal and mundane; school had God all over it. I just had to see it.

Whether you have chosen to be where you are or whether you feel you've just found yourself there, the Holy Spirit is at work, guiding and prompting you to be, act and speak as the light of Christ in that place.

You may not be like Paul in prison, but you might be constrained by the monotony of life or imprisoned in a job you can't see the end of or a way out from. Either way, this is the situation in which God wants to give you all that you need to be the best follower of Jesus. Through the Holy Spirit, he wants to give you the words you need and the strength you require to step out and step up in faith, integrity, love and grace, and to make you the best [*insert your own role here*] you can be.

THE PLACE WHERE WE ARE

Where have you been placed and what can you do?
Which of the circles in the diagram below feels like a
  prison?
Which feels monotonous?
Which seems to be an opportunity to share your faith
  and represent Jesus?

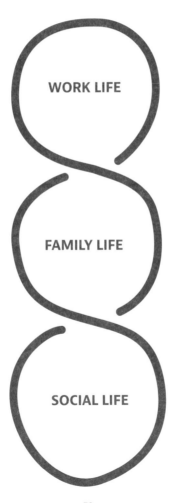

WORK LIFE

FAMILY LIFE

SOCIAL LIFE

YES, BUT HOW?

1 **Pray:** right now, pray for those you will meet today. Ask God to help you to show Jesus' love to them. If you can, take moments in the day to pray, remaining aware of God's presence and of those around you.

2 **Act:** take the opportunities that come your way to share God's love and to speak gently to those around you.

3 **Reflect:** tonight, celebrate those opportunities you took to share God's love. If you missed an opportunity, see it as a chance for growth – the next time a similar one arises, ask God to help you to take it.

PARTY ANIMAL OR LONE WOLF?

Q. 10: To what extent are you completely open and honest with one or two close friends about your strengths and failings?

> Perfume and incense bring joy to the heart,
>   and the pleasantness of a friend
>   springs from their heartfelt advice.
> (Proverbs 27.9)
>
> As iron sharpens iron,
>   so a friend sharpens a friend.
> (Proverbs 27.17 NLT)

When did you last confide in someone, bare all about a situation and ask for advice? Did you actually listen to the advice? Did you even choose to deal with the situation with that person's help instead of alone?

We live in an individualistic society, in which social media and hashtags such as #youdoyou #youareenough #justdoyou tell us that we are strong and independent, and that we don't need other people to be happy or to help us succeed. On the surface, this sounds very empowering and encouraging. But in a society in which up to 40 per cent of us report feeling lonely very often, this also seems to be extremely isolating. And it doesn't fit well with the picture of creation that the Bible paints.

The story of the Bible is a story of community, relationship and partnership but the effects of the fall were isolation, defensiveness and self-protection. God created us to be in deep, connected relationships but the introduction of the sin of pride pulled these relationships apart.

Let's reflect for a moment on Adam and Eve. God created these first humans to be in an intimate relationship, to work together and to strengthen and encourage each other. They were also to walk in the cool of the day with God – humans were designed to be with God in community. It wasn't until they sinned that isolation started to set in. We are told that the first thing Adam and Eve did after disobeying God was to try to hide their nakedness with fig leaves. Who were they hiding their private parts from? There were only the two of them and God. Sin always isolates us. Heaven's strategy is relationship; hell's strategy is isolation.

Later in the Bible, Jesus chose to work with his disciples and Paul worked with Timothy. In reality, Jesus could have done the miracles and preached the good news by himself. Instead, he chose to live out heaven's strategy and draw others into his circle. The disciples were a bunch of normal, broken, flawed humans who probably slowed things down, asked annoying questions and got in the way sometimes (or a lot). Jesus showed us the reality that it is better to work with other people, to go through life with other people, and to serve, struggle, win and fail with other people.

Jesus was not a lone wolf.

What would happen if we were to ignore social media and become more dependent on one another, talking, listening and collaborating more with our equally broken brothers and sisters? God designed us for partnership, relationship and family. We don't need to be lone wolves.

YES, BUT HOW?

QUESTIONS TO CONSIDER
- Who is the friend who is sharpening you?
- Are there people in your life you can share your faith/questions/problems/victories with?
- Could you invite a friend this week to sit and talk, perhaps over coffee? Why not take out your mobile and invite someone for a chat?

What do you need to be open and honest about with someone? (Fill in the boxes with your topics and name the items.)	Whom can you be honest with about this issue?
Mental health	
Physical health	
Worries and concerns	
Things to confess	

Anger	
Discussions you haven't had yet	

SATNAVS AND ROAD MAPS

Q. 15: Are you open to wrestling with and being challenged about things you believe?

> Your word is a lamp for my feet,
>   a light on my path.
> (Psalm 119.105)

My dad and I are so different. He loves a classic road atlas or street map and I love my satnav. If I want to go somewhere, I simply tap in the postcode, switch off my brain and let the Australian-accented voice direct me to my destination. My dad on the other hand pores over the atlas, working out his route and plotting his course. My tactic has not worked well for me in the long run – years have now passed and I still don't know the names of my local streets. Without my little box telling me what to do, I would have no idea how to find my way to a destination. My dad, on the other hand, has had years of learning road names and knows how to plot a course without his street map.

Which is the Bible like? A satnav or a street map?

The Bible is not meant to be something we read with our brains switched off. We're to wrestle with it, enjoy it and try to understand it. The Bible is a book to be engaged with and not just appreciated at a distance. The content of each page of the Bible is there to direct and teach us.

It helps us to navigate the landscape of a changing culture, like a map and compass. The Bible may not mention atom bombs but it does tell us about the sanctity of all life. Scripture deals with being human, and it directs us in the area of ethics, moral thinking, justice and the choices we make.

If you don't read the Bible, then how is God to direct your path and help you to navigate a morally changing world? As D. L. Moody once said, 'The Bible was not given to increase our knowledge; it was given to change our lives' (quoted in Rick Warren, *Bible Study Methods* (Zondervan, 2009), p. 16).

YES, BUT HOW?

- **Plan time to read it** The Bible needs some attention. It won't direct us as a satnav does. So set some time aside to look at it and give its content thought.
- **Find a quiet place** Give it your full attention. Don't try to read it when you're busy or distracted by other things.
- **Ask God to speak to you through it** Give God permission to direct your thinking as you read. Start by praying that God will make something clear for you or show you something that you need to see and understand.
- **Take time to chew on what you read. What does it mean and how does it apply?** Just as we would with a road map, we need to give thought to what the Bible says and ask ourselves how to apply it to our lives. Memorize a line and allow it to marinate inside you for the day. Is there something you are meant to understand in a deeper way?
- **Pray about what you have read** Ask God what he wants to say to you through the passage and give him

time to speak to you. He might be saying more than you imagine.

- **Put what you've learned into practice** Once you've found a good positive route through life's issues, you now have to act on it. It is often easier said than done.

Jesus said, 'Therefore everyone who hears these words of mine and puts them into practice is like a wise man who built his house on the rock' (Matthew 7.24). Activating the teaching of Jesus is a hard task because it's not always easy to see the direct connection with our lives without the help of others. A question I like to ask myself when trying to put a passage into practice is 'What changes today because I've read this passage?' This question helps me to think about how I might make the text a foundation for my day and how I can build my life on its teaching.

PRAYER

Loving God,
as I commit to read your word, meet me each step of the way.
Help me to learn to hear your voice through the Bible.
Show me how to make practical changes that will make me more like you.
Amen.

Q. 12: To what extent is your relationship with God being regularly cultivated and deepened?

[Jesus] said to them: 'It is not for you to know the times or dates the Father has set by his own authority. But you will receive power when the Holy Spirit comes on you; and you will be my witnesses in Jerusalem, and in all Judea and Samaria, and to the ends of the earth.'
(Acts 1.7–8)

I live in London, and there are many wonderful things about living in a city but, for me, there is one irritation. Pigeons. Pigeons are odd birds. Recently, as I sat in my kitchen, one flew directly into the window and knocked itself out. When I was on the Tube a year ago, a pigeon decided that it wanted to get into the train with everyone else, and it did. The train set off and the pigeon walked down the carriage looking for a seat. When the train arrived at the next stop, the pigeon politely walked out of the train and flew off. Once, when I was driving to Colchester, I ended up in a traffic jam and a pigeon landed on the bonnet of my car. It was like a scene from a horror film: it slowly turned its head until it revealed a weird, gammy eye. The one-eyed pigeon stared at me for 60 seconds, made a very strange noise and then flew off. You see what I mean? Pigeons are odd birds.

Pigeons are everywhere.
Pigeons are usually ignored by most city dwellers.
Pigeons are often hurt and have only half a wing, no foot or a weird eye.
Pigeons are wild and make a mess all over monuments.
With all that said, pigeons make effective messengers.

In Matthew 3.16, we read that 'As soon as Jesus was baptised, he went up out of the water. At that moment heaven was opened, and he saw the Spirit of God descending like a dove and alighting on him.' Let's talk about doves. Doves are remote, we don't see them often, they are seen as angelic birds, they are beautiful – the *Baywatch* of birds, if you will. If you imagine the Holy Spirit as a dove, you will see him as remote, distant, unattainable and otherworldly. The Holy Spirit is not a dove. The Holy Spirit is more like a pigeon than a dove. The Holy Spirit is normal but a little bit weird.

We are told that the *peristera* descended on Jesus. Most Bibles give the translation of this Greek word as 'dove'. Actually, though, it can be translated a 'pigeon'. Some Middle Eastern versions of the Bible actually do so.

Like pigeons, the Holy Spirit is everywhere.
Like pigeons, he is usually ignored.
Like pigeons, the Holy Spirit can be hurt (don't grieve the Holy Spirit).
Like pigeons, the Holy Spirit is wild and can make a mess.
Like a pigeon, he is an effective messenger.

The Holy Spirit is not a dove but a pigeon, which is really important for so many of us. The Holy Spirit is normal, he is knowable, he lives with and in you, and he makes God present. He is your greatest champion, who speaks for you as a defence lawyer.

This Holy Pigeon comes to rest upon God's people to empower them to do and see the kinds of things Jesus taught about, practised and encouraged. Each of the disciples received the same Holy Pigeon as Jesus, so that they might become radical carriers of the good news.

YES, BUT HOW?

Jesus told the disciples, '*Do not leave* Jerusalem, but *wait* for the gift my Father promised, which you have heard me speak about' (Acts 1.4). To encounter the Holy Spirit, Jesus tells us to

1   stop (do not)
2   pause (leave)
3   wait (wait for the gift).

Take some time each day to stop and wait for the Holy Spirit. Many of us don't feel anything extraordinary; receiving the Spirit is as normal as it comes. Each day, if you invite God to fill you with the Spirit, he will. Even if you don't sense it, God wants to share his presence with you. Once you have asked to be filled, walk in the Spirit. Look for opportunities to live in tune with the Holy Spirit. With the Spirit can come many gifts, such as those shown on the right. Look for ways to practise those gifts God gives you. The more you use them, the more they will become second nature.

BEING EMPOWERED BY THE HOLY SPIRIT

CARING HEART   PEACE   KNOWLEDGE   GENEROSITY

MIRACLES   HEALING   UNDERSTANDING

WISDOM   COURAGE   ENCOURAGEMENT   PROPHECY

COUNSEL   GODLY REVERENCE   LEADERSHIP

FAITH   TONGUES   ADMINISTRATION   AND MORE

PRAYER

Father,

Thank you for the glory of your words and obedience to
   your commandments.

Grant me the power of the Holy Spirit to teach your words
   with increased wisdom, knowledge and understanding.

Empower my **mind** to think like yours,

   my **heart** to be passionate like yours,

   and my **hands** to serve, care and heal, so that I may be
   like your Son Jesus.

Amen.

DAY 16
MAKE YOUR YES A YES

Q. 14: How much of an impact do your beliefs and the Bible have on your attitude towards culture, the world and your community?

Again, you have heard that it was said to the people long ago, 'Do not break your oath, but fulfil to the Lord the vows you have made.' But I tell you, do not swear an oath at all: either by heaven, for it is God's throne; or by the earth, for it is his footstool; or by Jerusalem, for it is the city of the Great King. And do not swear by your head, for you cannot make even one hair white or black. All you need to say is simply 'Yes,' or 'No'; anything beyond this comes from the evil one.
(Matthew 5.33–37)

As the musician Jack Johnson sings on his track 'Flake', 'maybe' nearly always means 'no'. In recent years, society seems to have changed its definition of commitment. Divorce is not uncommon, employees no longer join a company for life but for a season, and people are much more likely to change their group affiliations because of single issues.

One place that this is most evident is on social media.

If you are invited to an event through a well-known social media platform, you are given three options for responding: 'yes', 'no' and 'maybe'. Selecting 'maybe' means there's a possibility that you might attend, but you are not fully committed and you retain the right to reconsider nearer the time. Therefore, if you do something else, you are not letting the host down because you didn't officially say 'yes' in the first place. Recently, I was involved with an event where a page was created on the platform. People were invited to come along and were given the usual options to respond: 'yes', 'no' and 'maybe'. Many people selected 'maybe' and then didn't show up on the night. When the organizer asked an invitee why he or she couldn't come, the person said, 'I couldn't make it. I just wanted to be polite and show interest, but I never had any intention of coming.'

- 'Maybe' has become a way of responding to be polite and to avoid the discomfort of saying 'no'.
- 'Maybe' allows room for uncertainty and leaves people wondering if we are dependable.
- 'Maybe' feeds a personality that thrives on an attitude of 'I'll see how I feel on the night'.
- 'Maybe' allows us to accept a better, later offer and not feel guilty about rejecting the first invitation.

Jesus said that we should simply be 'yes' or 'no' people. As disciples, we are challenged to show our cards, to ensure that others can see our strength of character through commitment. Jesus calls us to make commitments. Through committing to love one another, we demonstrate God's commitment to others by playing our part in community life.

When Jesus gave his teaching on oaths or vows, he spoke into a specific cultural issue of his day. People had developed an unhelpful practice of swearing on holy or precious items to do things, which required them to prove their promises and which weren't based on personal integrity. For example, they would say things like, 'I make a promise on the altar of the temple' or 'I make a promise on heaven'. Today, we might hear people say 'I make a pinky promise' or 'I swear on my mother's grave'. Jesus wanted to challenge this behaviour because he wanted his disciples to be known for integrity. What you say should stand without requiring an extra, binding oath.

We have to push back at this culture of 'maybe'. Are you known as someone who makes a commitment and follows through? We live in a culture which accepts that people are 'flaky' when it comes to commitments. But in Romans 12.10 it says, 'Be devoted to one another in love. Honour one another above yourselves.'

Let's practise honouring others by making and keeping our commitments.

YES, BUT HOW?

Make a pledge to practise not using the words 'maybe', 'perhaps' and 'possibly'. When an opportunity comes up and you need to make a commitment, simply let your answer be 'yes' or 'no'. If you decide to say no but think the situation might change, keep your intentions clear by saying, 'If anything changes, I will let you know.'

If you have an event in your diary but someone or something better comes along, keep your original commitment. Show the person who first invited you how much you are committed to them by sticking to your plans.

Is there anything that you need to rectify today because you have either let someone down or not made a commitment? Is there a person to ask for forgiveness? Is there something to make right?

PRAYER

Father,

I thank you that you have made a commitment to me.

No matter what I do, you never let go of this commitment.

When my commitment is shaky, help me to take
responsibility to make my response a firm 'yes'.

When I let people down, help me to find space to repent
and make it right.

When I still struggle to commit, please send your Holy
Spirit to work to form me into your likeness.

Today, may my yes be yes.

Amen.

FROM TENANTS TO OWNERS

Q. 7: How much are your daily habits changing to reflect God's care for his creation?

God blessed them and said to them, 'Be fruitful and increase in number; fill the earth and subdue it. Rule over the fish in the sea and the birds in the sky and over every living creature that moves on the ground.'
(Genesis 1.28)

When I first moved to London, I noticed that there was a much higher number of people who rent rooms or homes. People under a certain age don't tend to own property in the city; it's not financially possible for so many. Friends rent flats with four or five other friends to make living in London possible. I have come across my share of poor, absentee landlords, and tenants who had left homes in a mess because they were moving on and didn't care about who came next. I know friends who have rented flats only to find that, before they could move in with their own possessions, they had to throw out 20 to 30 black sacks of belongings left behind by someone else.

Sometimes, as Christians, we behave as if we rent a room on planet Earth and God, our landlord, isn't bothered about how we leave it, so long as we pay our rent! Our 'real home' is in heaven, we think. This idea of mass evacuation to some heavenly upgrade post death comes more from Greek myth than from the Bible. The Bible speaks more about heaven coming to earth and the restoration of all things, rather than the idea that we go to a hotel in the sky. Because of this misunderstanding, we end up not really worrying about the state we leave our room in; we just do what we want with the world.

What about these things – destructive farming practices, overproduction of single-use plastics, the unhindered burning of fossil fuels in factories and by cars and aeroplanes? The verses we have today from Genesis paint another picture. They show us that humanity was created in the 'image of God' and he asked us to 'fill the earth'. The truth is that we are already home. We aren't just renting; we share in God's ownership of this world.

Caring for creation is at the heart of the gospel. The first command was for us to care for creation, but sin entered the world because humans ate the apple and our relationship with God, one another and the planet was badly undermined. Jesus' death and resurrection not only reclaim the relationship between us and God but also that between others and the planet. All this takes us back to the original partnership found in Genesis 1 and Genesis 3.

When we have a sense of ownership over the place we call 'home', when we care about its condition, we are happy to invest time and money to make it a place of joy to live in. When we own the place we live in, we have to deal with the problems involved in nurturing and caring for that space. If we, as mature homeowners, don't sort problems out, no one else will.

We are called to 'subdue' and 'rule' creation, as owners with God. Our 'ruling' is to share in his rule, and God's rule is ultimately made known to us through Jesus. He loves creation so much that he entered the world, coming to serve rather than be served – dying to bring life, flourishing and fullness, and rising again to rule, so that freedom might win.

God uses his power by becoming powerless; God rules through service, and we are made in his image. Tied up in the essence of what it means to be human is the need to care and serve the world we have been given. How do you care for creation? Can you care for creation?

YES, BUT HOW?

Notice the world around you: people, places, streets, buildings, life. Notice beauty and notice pain.
Dream of what it would be like for these places to flourish. What might 'ruling' – caring, nurturing – look like here?
Do something practical to love better the place where you are.

NOTICE   DREAM   DO

DAY 18
ROCK BOTTOM

Q. 10: To what extent are you completely open and honest with one or two close friends about your strengths and failings?

Unless the LORD had given me help,
    I would soon have dwelt in the silence of death.
When I said, 'My foot is slipping,'
    your unfailing love, LORD, supported me.
When anxiety was great within me,
    your consolation brought me joy.
(Psalm 94.17–19)

I have a good friend who was a drug addict for 14 years. He even moved to the UK to try to hide his addiction from his family. He recently said to me:

I have experienced in life what many call 'rock bottom'. It's interesting – for 13 years, my family wanted me to do something that I didn't want to do myself: to stop taking drugs. For those 13 years, my mother prayed numerous times that God would intervene and prevent me from dying or going to jail. The more my mother prayed, the worse my situation became. I started to lose jobs, friends and, in the end, I nearly lost my soul. In Psalm 94.19, it says, 'When anxiety was great within me, your consolation brought me joy.' When it was great within *me*, not with my mother or sister or partner. I needed to hit rock bottom to be able to surrender and to accept God's consolation.

Before many of us can find any sense of freedom about any issue, we have to hit rock bottom, where we realize that we can't make a lasting change without God's help.

I heard a story of a woman who was a recovering alcoholic, who would go into a prison to share her journey through recovery with the inmates. While sharing one day, she said to a room full of tattooed, drug-addicted prisoners, 'If I could give you all the gift of recovery, I wouldn't do it.'

Upset, the convicts asked (with expletives deleted), 'Why are you so mean?'

Her response was brilliant: 'Because I don't want to rob you of your journey.'

There is a danger, when we are struggling, depressed or anxious, that we will say, 'I will pray for God's help.' But the truth is that there are two 'parts' to freedom. Our part and God's part. We need the Spirit of God *and* we need people we can be honest with to start to find freedom. What we don't 'talk out' we will always act out. The need to have one other person with whom to share is central for finding full freedom. It doesn't matter what our problem is, money, sex, friendships, gambling, prescription drugs or anxiety, until we allow the Spirit of God and good wise people to help us, we cannot find full freedom. If you are your own mentor, you have a bad mentor. Proverbs 16.25 tells us, 'There is a way that appears to be right, but in the end it leads to death.' Without good friendships and wise support, our best intentions will always be distorted by our own opinions. We need others who have been where we are to help us get out of the hole.

There was once a man struggling with his reliance on prescription drugs who fell into a deep hole. A lawyer walked past and heard the man's cry for help. The lawyer was concerned for the guy. He said, 'I'll make some calls; I'll send a few emails; I will see what I can do.' Before he walked away, he dropped a business card into the hole.

Next, a priest passed by and heard the man's cry for help. 'I will say a prayer for you, brother,' he said and walked on.

Finally, another man came along, heard the man's cry for help and jumped into the hole. The man who had fallen into the hole was furious. 'Why did you do that?! Now we are both are stuck! At least you could have dropped a rope down to me.'

The other man looked at him and said, 'I've been here; I know the way out.'

We need to open up, be honest and look for people to say the same to us: 'I've been here; I know the way out.'

YES, BUT HOW?

Whatever your destructive behaviour might be, is it bad enough for you to want to make a change that leads to freedom? Have you come to realize that you are defenceless without a Christian community and the Holy Spirit?

What is the internal battle you have lost? What do you have to admit, so that God can then enter the ring to fight for you? For you, it may not be any of the examples given in today's thought, but we all have something that's struggling to control us. What is it for you? Can you give this to God today and let someone else in?

PRAYER

Jesus,
grant me the serenity to accept the things I cannot change,
courage to change the things I can,
and wisdom to know the difference.
Amen.

DO YOU INFLUENCE OR ARE YOU INFLUENCED?

Q. 1: How much of your day-to-day life changes as you think about what it means to live for Jesus?

Since, then, you have been raised with Christ, set your hearts on things above, where Christ is, seated at the right hand of God. Set your minds on things above, not on earthly things. For you died, and your life is now hidden with Christ in God.
(Colossians 3.1–3)

As many people do, I have a hobby that I really enjoy and which brings me life. It means that I spend time and many days off with people of little or no faith. After I'd been at a club for the hobby for a couple of years or so, one of the members approached me and said, 'It's so lovely when you are out with us. There is always far less foul language and people don't argue as much when you are around. Everyone is much more light-hearted when you are here.' I truly appreciated the comment, but not fully until I got home. I don't know what it's like when I'm not with the guys; I only know what it's like when I am there. For someone to comment on the difference my presence makes really got me thinking.

One of the key questions of life that I've been asked is this: are you a **thermometer** or a **thermostat**? Just in case you're not sure what the difference is, a thermometer *measures* the temperature that's already there – whether it's the fever that you've developed or the warmth of your living room. A thermostat, on the other hand, *sets* the temperature; it controls, in some super-technical way, how cool or warm a space is going to be. In other words, a thermometer *indicates* the temperature; a thermostat *regulates* the temperature.

Some of us, whether we are followers of Jesus or not, are definitely more like thermometers. If everything around us is negative, cynical or critical, then we are affected and we become similar because we pick up the culture around us. We allow it to mould us and shape our thoughts and attitudes. Nevertheless, we are not called to be thermometers. Rather, we are to take our attitudes and behaviour from what we read in the Bible, and to choose to set our minds on Jesus and the things that matter the most to him. Then we can begin to set the temperature, as thermostats do, even to change the temperature around us, in our homes, workplaces, leisure activities, on our streets and in our neighbourhoods.

Because Jesus is truth, integrity and authenticity matter to us.

Because he is love, treating everyone with respect and valuing each person matters to us.

Because he is holy, living in a pure way that pleases God matters to us.

Because he is faithful, being committed, trustworthy, reliable and faithful in our relationships matters to us.

YES, BUT HOW?

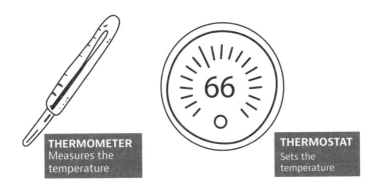

THERMOMETER
Measures the
temperature

THERMOSTAT
Sets the
temperature

A thermometer or a thermostat?

- Which are you in your home?
- Which are you in your workplace?
- Which are you in your social life?
- Which are you in your church?

Take time today to be aware of what is going on around you. Are you more influenced by those in the room or by Jesus?

Ask yourself how you can begin to set a more 'Jesus-centred' temperature where you are.

STANDING ON THE SHOULDERS OF JESUS

Q. 4: To what extent are you helping others to serve God better?

Very truly I tell you, whoever believes in me will do the works I have been doing, and they will do even greater things than these, because I am going to the Father. And I will do whatever you ask in my name, so that the Father may be glorified in the Son. You may ask me for anything in my name, and I will do it.
(John 14.12–14)

I love this quote by the author and motivational speaker, Zig Ziglar: 'A lot of people have gone further than they thought they could because someone else thought they could' (quoted in David Dwight, Terry Grapentine and David Soorholtz, *Critical Thinking for Marketers*, volume II (Business Expert Press, 2016), p. 163).

We all hope to have someone in our lives who will help us go further and do more than we imagine we can. Having a champion to cheer us on, celebrate us and encourage us is a part of being human. Without such a person in our lives, we may never fully appreciate all that we could be.

We also need to be that sort of individual for others. I love the phrase 'standing on the shoulders of giants'.

Apparently, Sir Isaac Newton said, 'If I have seen further, it is by standing on the shoulders of giants.' I have been privileged to stand on the shoulders of some amazing people of God, who gave me opportunities to try new things, make mistakes and learn. If those people, who held positions of influence, hadn't allowed me to learn from them, I would never have been able to develop and grow in the way that I have. Here's a challenge for us all: do we want to hold on to the power and influence that we now have, or do we want to hand them on to the next generation? As we stand on the shoulders of giants, so we need to let others stand on ours.

Sometimes we try to hold on to our power and influence; sometimes we want to make a name for ourselves; sometimes we want to be highly thought of. This behaviour will always leave us with a finite amount of influence. To have the greatest influence is to let go and let others thrive on the back of our learning, wisdom and experience.

Jesus recognized that his disciples were going to do the works that he had been doing, and that they would 'do even greater things'. Jesus passed on his ministry to the next generation. He knew that his mission would reach the ends of the earth and have an impact on billions of lives but, for it to do so, he had to hand it on to the next generation, who were empowered by the Holy Spirit. If Jesus had held on to his ministry, he would have affected only a small number of people in the Middle East. By handing it on to others, however, he ensured that the message passed like a virus from person to person.

If we take Jesus as our blueprint for life, we see him apprenticing his followers right from the very start. He builds up their confidence, involves them in problem-solving, sends them off to try what they have seen him do, gives feedback and then hands his work on to them. Our role as disciples of Jesus is to do the same. We are to become people who are willing to help others to serve God better by coaching, holding them and encouraging them. Too often our faith becomes an insular thing, but the call of Jesus in our lives is to be people who set others free to serve God and serve their neighbours.

YES, BUT HOW?

QUESTIONS TO CONSIDER

- Whom can you allow to stand on your shoulders?
- Who are you, or could you be, intentionally helping to serve God better?
- What skills, gifts or knowledge can you hand on to someone else?

- What are your worries about doing so?
- Do you fear losing out on something?

REFLECTION

Take some time to think about whose shoulders you stand on and who stands on yours.

PRAYER

Father,

thank you for those who have allowed me to stand on their shoulders, as I have grown in faith.

I thank you for their humility, faith, hope and courage.

I thank you that they have seen me for what I could be and not what I was.

Today, I thank you for [*name(s)*].

And now I pray for those who stand on my shoulders.

Please help me to have the same humility, faith, hope and courage as those who have gone before me.

Help me to invest in them, encourage them, cheer them on and show them the beauty of who they are.

Today, I thank you for [*name(s)*], who trust(s) me to carry them.

And I pray for those I have yet to allow to stand on my shoulders.

Give me the humility to invite them to allow me to serve them in this way.

Amen.

DAY 21
ARE YOU WILLING TO BE TAUGHT?

Q. 16: To what extent are you allowing yourself to learn from those who think differently from you?

Why do you call me, 'Lord, Lord,' and do not do what I say? As for everyone who comes to me and hears my words and puts them into practice, I will show you what they are like. They are like a man building a house, who dug down deep and laid the foundation on rock. When the flood came, the torrent struck that house but could not shake it, because it was well built. But the one who hears my words and does not put them into practice is like a man who built a house on the ground without a foundation. The moment the torrent struck that house, it collapsed and its destruction was complete.
(Luke 6.46–49)

A friend of mine is a teacher in a secondary school in east London. As many teachers do, he finds that he repeats himself over and over again. At the end of a maths class, he saw that one of his pupils was feeling sorry for herself and was slumped over her desk. She wasn't there for being badly behaved but because, as she had been reminded many times before, sending offensive messages on social media has real-life consequences. The schoolgirl, as at other times, simply nodded at him and nursed her bruised face and pride, promising that next time would be different. As I talked the incident through with my friend, I saw the pain on his face as he said, 'Why won't they listen? Can't they see my advice is for their own good?'

The truth is that many of us are exactly like that teenager. Are we teachable or do we really think we know best? A while ago, I was showing a church member how to run some new software that we were trying out before a service. Following every point I made, he would say, 'Yes, I know that.' Feeling confident, I left him to run the software but quickly found that his confidence in himself was less than accurate. He had no idea and shouldn't have been left alone at the computer. He was not teachable, and continued in this manner over subsequent weeks.

In today's reading, Jesus tells the wonderful story about wise and foolish builders. By way of a short introduction, he says, 'Why do you call me, "Lord, Lord," and do not do what I say?' We hear the good news; we look at what Jesus tells us in the Bible and we promise that life is going to change. But a week passes, life gets busy and we find ourselves building on sandy foundations once again.

Jesus is the ultimate teacher but will we listen? Do we sometimes believe, deep down, like the pupil in the classroom or the person with the new software, that Jesus doesn't have our best interests at heart? We have to be honest here. We need to ask Jesus to speak to our hearts and help us to understand that he teaches us so that we can have life to the full. And then we need to hear the word of God and put it into practice. We have to be willing to be taught and willing to change, replacing our shaky foundations with the unchanging truth of Jesus.

YES, BUT HOW?

How willing are you to allow the teachings of Jesus to really change your life?

1 **I find it helpful to read a Bible passage with someone else** We can discuss what speaks to us, chat about one thing that we might do more often or something we might change in our daily lives. We can then commit to praying for each other and challenging each other about whether we've put the goals we agreed into practice.

2 **Always leave the Bible with a next step** Remember what Jesus said: it's not enough merely to hear the word of God, we have to put it into practice. And that's why the phrase 'next step' is so important. When you read the Bible, don't just ask, 'What does God want me to know?' You also need to ask 'What does God want me to do?' Before you move on from reading the Bible, try writing down what your small or large next step is. By writing it down, it will become something to remember and do. Every passage of the Bible has something in it to inspire us to act.

3 **Celebrate the little wins** It is important to be able to see the progress we make no matter how small it is. It's easy to be disappointed in your progress but it can be powerful to see where you have come from. Make sure you celebrate those next steps that you have activated. This can be much easier to do when talking it through with others.

QUESTIONS TO CONSIDER

- What do you need to put into practice today because you read this passage?
- What is your next step?

PRAYER

Lord our God,

in your wisdom and love, you surround us with the mysteries of the universe.

Pour out your Spirit on me and fill me with your wisdom and blessings.

Grant that I may devote myself to your teaching and draw ever closer to you, the source of all knowledge.

Help me to be teachable today, slow in believing I know it all and quick to listen.

I ask this through Jesus Christ our Lord.

Amen.

DAY 22
MAKE IT LESS ABOUT YOU

Q. 2: How committed are you to local church community?

For even the Son of Man did not come to be served, but to serve, and to give his life as a ransom for many.
(Mark 10.45)

A fatberg – a congealed mass of flushed items in a sewer system – sat beneath the London streets growing for many years, weighing the same as at least 11 double-decker buses, full of wipes, cooking oil and other 'necessities' that we had thrown down our toilets or waste disposal units. It reeked of today's consumer culture. We want it all and we want it now. Society shows us that the more we have, the more entitled we will feel to have things, therefore the greater our desire will be for even more.

We often carry this attitude into church. What will I get from church today? Is the talk giving me enough? There is a story of two men leaving church one Sunday morning.

'I didn't get much from the service today – the worship was flat and the sermon was dull,' said one to the other, before they got to the bottom of the church steps.

'I didn't know the worship was for you,' the second man replied.

We worship God not because we get anything from it but because he deserves our praise.

This verse in Mark provides a huge challenge to our individualistic and often self-centred attitudes. We are told that even Jesus, God himself, came to earth to serve others. He came to earth asking not what he was going to receive, but what he was going to give. The verse then takes this idea even further when it says that Jesus came not only to serve but also 'to give his life as a ransom for many'. Jesus came to give his life – the ultimate model of sacrificial love – so that we could be free.

Coming to church to be blessed and to hear God speak is not a bad thing; it is so important to experience God as part of a community of believers. But it is also about becoming more like Jesus. This verse tells us exactly what this looks like: we enter church and we live each day with an attitude of service.

Sadly, just as the fatberg under the streets of London tells the story of a city gripped by consumerism, our lives tell the story of our relationship with God. Are we free from materialism or is our fatberg rotting with the stench of narcissistic me-centred worship, decaying with Bible reading that is about what we get, not what we give, and leaden with the weight of prayerlessness?

I often ask myself, is Christ the centre of my faith or is Cris?

QUESTIONS YOU ASK YOURSELF WHEN YOU COME TO CHURCH

Notice the questions you ask yourself when you come to church: are they focused on you or on God?

- Will I like the worship songs?

- Will I enjoy the talk?
- Will the coffee be any good this week?

Consider replacing them with one of the following questions this coming week:

- Could I get to know someone new today?
- Is there someone on the edge whom I could involve in a conversation?
- Does anyone need help looking after their children?
- Could I get someone a cup of tea or coffee?
- How can I help today?
- Is God asking anything of me today?
- Did I really adore God today or was I distracted?

SONG

Why not watch the song 'Nothing else' by Cody Carnes online or download it? The lyrics are beautiful; the song talks about coming to worship with the wrong agenda. Through the lyrics, the songwriter invites us to say sorry for just going through the motions and for singing worship songs mindlessly without fixing our eyes on God. He encourages us to turn our full attention, without our own agenda, to Jesus.

PRAYER

Less of the drama,
   less of my selfishness,
   less of my complaining,
   less of the bitterness,
   less of the gossip,
   less of the pride,
   less of the anger,
   less of me . . .

   . . . more of you, Jesus.

Jesus, I step out of the way and allow you to fill the room.
Jesus, I get out of the driving seat and let you direct and set the course.
Jesus, I come to take less and wonder more at your beauty, majesty and glory.
King Jesus, I pray today for more of you in my life and less of me;
   increase my hunger for your presence.
Teach me to depend on you and you alone.
Holy Spirit, fill me and trigger in me the desire to listen to you and do what you ask today.
Help me to leave aside anything in my life that is blocking my thirst for God in Jesus' name.
Amen.

DAY 23
WHAT IS SHAPING YOU?

Q. 14: How much of an impact do your beliefs and the Bible have on your attitude towards culture, the world and your community?

> Yet you, LORD, are our Father.
>> We are the clay, you are the potter;
>> we are all the work of your hand.
> (Isaiah 64.8)

From a young age, my kids loved playing with modelling dough. They would sit for many hours enjoying the bright colours and the silly things that they could make. Many times, they would sculpt a model that they wanted to keep. It would be placed on the mantelpiece and left to gather dust. It would be knocked or bumped, and slowly it would fall into disrepair, easily reshaped by accidental damage.

The world we live in isn't easy to navigate, and we don't live lives wrapped in cotton wool. The knocks and bumps of life will damage what we don't protect. Isaiah 64 refers to us as lumps of clay that God wants to mould and sculpt. There are many things in our lives that influence our shape: whom we spend time with, how we use our resources and where we visit. Some influences are life-giving, but some are not helpful and will cause distortion and harm.

Our minds can be unconsciously shaped by silent influences. People aren't born racist, prejudiced, cynical, greedy and so on. We are moulded by silent influences more than we realize. What we consume and who surrounds us will shape us. We are bombarded by thousands of adverts each day, which we pass without consciously noticing. We are formed by the quiet views of family, friends and colleagues more than we are aware.

As followers of Jesus, we have to ask ourselves whether Jesus is our main influence. Does the Bible have a greater impact on our lives than *Cosmopolitan* magazine or the *Daily Mail*? Are we even aware of what is shaping us? Who has the greatest influence over your way of thinking? Romans 12.2 reminds us not to be sculpted by this world but to be transformed by the reshaping of our thinking. By this, we will be able to work out what is God's good and perfect will.

My family and I go camping most summers on the south coast of England, where we have perfect access to the sea for surfing. Our tent is a five-minute walk from the beach, which is exposed to the full brunt of the weather and waves. Every tree on that coast has been permanently bent by the wind continually coming off the sea. Not one of them is upright. This is what Paul was speaking of when he wrote, 'Do not grow bent under the pressure of the wind, but be upright because of God's scaffolding' (Romans 12.2, my version).

YES, BUT HOW?

1 **Awareness** Be honest with yourself. What do you watch, read or listen to that influences your thinking more than you like? How does this compare with

the amount of input from God? Being aware of what shapes you is the first step.

2 **Course correct** 'You are what you are and where you are because of what has gone into your mind. You can change what you are and where you are by changing what goes into your mind' (Zig Ziglar, *Raising Positive Kids in a Negative World* (CD series, 1988)).

Before you read the Bible, always pray for its words to shape you. Assume every passage has something to say about the way you should think or behave. Ask yourself the question, 'Which "course correction" do I need to make, to make sure that I am heading in God's direction for my day?'

SET A GOAL

Right now, why not take a moment to ask God how he wants to shape your thinking today. Ask for a practical thing he wants you to think differently about, then spend the day actively moving in that direction. Alongside God's guidance, we need the willingness and courage to change – make sure you pray and ask God for his help and support.

PRAYER

Father,
I declare right now that you have the right
to interfere in my life any time, in any way,
for you are the potter and I am the clay.
Amen.

DAY 24
A BIGGER WORLD

Q. 18: To what extent are you regularly discovering more about Jesus and his work in our world?

The land yields its harvest;
    God, our God, blesses us.
May God bless us still,
    so that all the ends of the earth will fear him.
(Psalm 67.6–7)

Do you remember those 'What Would Jesus Do?' bracelets that people wore? They were big in the Christian world in the late 1990s. I not only had the WWJD fabric band on my wrist but also the PUSH (Pray Until Something Happens) and FROG (Fully Rely On God) bands, just to make sure people knew that I was taking my faith seriously. At my school, we weren't allowed to wear jewellery unless there was a religious reason for it. A friend and I were told to remove our bracelets because they went against the school uniform code. We thought of this as a persecution of our faith; we loudly stated that they were symbols of our Christian belief and that we would not remove them.

A few years later, I heard about Christians who had been locked up in shipping containers for their faith; the lack of sunlight made their hair and teeth fall out. I heard of others who were sent to forced labour camps, imprisoned without trial and even murdered. A couple of years ago, I was able to visit refugee camps on the border between Syria and Lebanon. There, I was told about women raped for their faith, children burnt for their faith and men murdered for their faith.

Suddenly my WWJD bracelet didn't seem very significant. I was learning about people all over the globe for whom declaring the name of Jesus could cost them everything, and yet they still did it. Individuals smuggled Bibles across borders, held secret church services, baptized new believers and never gave up their faith in the face of death. And even more captivating were the stories of God's moving: how he would make border control guards almost blind, so that they wouldn't see a boot full of illegal Bibles; how he made prison doors open, so captives could walk out of maximum-security units; and how he gave people supernatural strength to withstand terrible ordeals.

What we experience in the West is persecution, but it isn't anywhere near the level that other brothers and sisters experience every single day. In 2017, I had the honour of meeting Hea Woo, a North Korean woman who had been imprisoned in a labour camp for her Christian faith. She shared an incredible testimony of planting a church in that North Korean labour camp. She and the other women could meet for church only in the queue for the toilet and could sing worship songs only when it was raining to hide their voices. Her testimony made me think about my commitment to Jesus. Do I live my faith with the same conviction as others do under persecution?

In 2018, I met a Syrian pastor (see Day 11, p. 52). He shared with me what it was like to be a Christian in Syria at that time and it frightened me. Not because of what he said about Syria but because of what it said about my faith. He told me:

> The war was a gift; it made us wake up to the reality that humanity is lost without Jesus . . . I've seen many survive persecution but not many survive prosperity . . . You are more in love with life than you are with Jesus, and it makes you unwilling to die for him . . . There is a satanic lullaby over the [Western] Church; it's as if you are falling asleep.

I share this again because it's a wake-up call to the reality that Christians are living through great times of persecution. Not only that, those Christians can see persecution very differently from us. How serious are we for Jesus? Are we asleep? Jesus said, 'If you want to be my disciple, pick up your cross and follow me' (Luke 9.23, my version). How willing are we to die for Jesus?

YES, BUT HOW

Learning about Christians around the world, and how life-giving and sustaining their faith is in such circumstances, encouraged and challenged me in mine. If you've never looked beyond your own church, then why not check out Open Doors <www.opendoorsuk.org> and let your Jesus family around the world encourage and challenge you today. You might also want to think about:

- writing letters of encouragement to those who are persecuted – visit: <www.opendoorsuk.org/act/letter>;

- taking action to support those who are persecuted – Open Doors suggests a number of ways to do so at: <www.opendoorsuk.org/act>.

PRAYER

Finally, spend some time in prayer. Ask for the passion and love for Jesus found in the persecuted Church to awaken your faith and passion for him too.

When my faith is asleep, awake my soul.
When my commitment to you is second, awake my soul.
When I am holding on to this world, awake my soul.
When my faith is more of a hobby than a commitment, awake my soul.
When I am fearful of being found out, awake my soul.
Amen.

THE MINISTRY OF THE WEAK

Q. 4: To what extent are you helping others to serve God better?

But he said to me, 'My grace is sufficient for you, for my power is made perfect in weakness.' Therefore I will boast all the more gladly about my weaknesses, so that Christ's power may rest on me. That is why, for Christ's sake, I delight in weaknesses, in insults, in hardships, in persecutions, in difficulties. For when I am weak, then I am strong.
(2 Corinthians 12.9–11)

There is something really wrong in some models of church and making disciples. Often those who are thought to be strong minister to those who are thought to be weak. The wealthy help the poor; the healthy help the sick; the older help the young; the educated help the ignorant; the mended help the broken; and the gifted help the needy. Because of these attitudes, we often look at our own lives and realize that we aren't strong, healthy, wealthy, wise, know-it-all or gifted, so we wait until we are. Thus a few special, confident individuals serve a growing number of people looking for what they lack. Those who are presumed to have it all tell those who presume to have nothing how to get everything.

Even the way we tell testimonies about what God has done feed into this elitist way of thinking. We celebrate and rejoice when a problem is fixed, a disease is healed, a child is born, a debt is paid, a job is found, a wedding has happened, and so on and so forth. We elevate blessing and therefore assume that the receiver of the blessing is somehow better than we are. This situation leaves some of us feeling like works in progress. If our stories are that God is working on us but we aren't finished yet, that God is elbow deep in filth, head in the engine trying to work out the problem, then we think we have nothing to offer. It's as if we believe that we can only help others when the wound is healed, not while our arms are in slings.

So, with this as the backdrop, we end up with superstar pastors and ministers, who may have huge numbers of people following *them* rather than Christ. But there is good news: the story of God is the story of the wounded leading the wounded and the poor leading the poor. God didn't come to us as a mighty leader but as a fragile baby, which is God's way.

Jesus isn't known for strength but for humility.
Jesus healed us not by being a mighty warrior but through his death.
Jesus did not save us by the power of his crown but by his powerlessness on the cross.

We have this odd idea that we can't help others until we have everything wrapped up and sorted. The disciples of Jesus were certainly ministering before they were ready, which is why they made so many mistakes and Jesus had to keep repeating himself. God does not wait for us to finish a course, a degree or a qualification before he uses us. Our saying 'yes' to Jesus is our qualification.

YES, BUT HOW?

I was first discipled by twin brothers, John and James, who were two years older – I was 15 and they were 17. They spoke into my life, they took me places with them to experience things, and they prayed with me. They told me what they were learning and helped me to discover who I was in my faith. They were only two years older than I was but they were among the most significant voices in my life.

Think about, discover and, like my friends, the twin brothers, offer what you have.

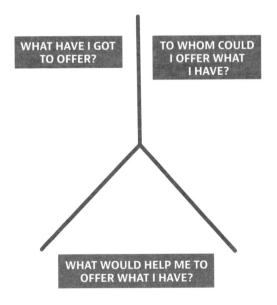

WHAT HAVE I GOT TO OFFER?

TO WHOM COULD I OFFER WHAT I HAVE?

WHAT WOULD HELP ME TO OFFER WHAT I HAVE?

QUESTIONS TO CONSIDER

- Can you help someone else on his or her faith journey?
- Can you give someone else your time to show him or her how to do something?
- Can you invite someone to do something with you so that you can show that person the ropes?
- In whom can you start to invest?
- Who is a short distance behind? Can you give that person your time?

PRAYER

Help me not to wait to be strong before strengthening the weak.

Help me to be generous in my poverty as well as with my wealth.

Help me not to wait until I know enough to get involved.

Make me an instrument of your work today.

Amen.

DAY 26
DON'T BE SPOON-FED, FIND OUT FOR YOURSELF: ALLOW THE BIBLE TO FORM YOU

Q. 14: How much of an impact do your beliefs and the Bible have on your attitude towards culture, the world and your community?
Q. 17: How much time do you regularly spend engaging with the Bible?

Now the Berean Jews were of more noble character than those in Thessalonica, for they received the message with great eagerness and examined the Scriptures every day to see if what Paul said was true.
(Acts 17.11)

One of the messiest tasks I have ever had was trying to spoon-feed my 15-month-old daughter with tomato-based baby food. We both ended up covered in the food; so did the kitchen walls, floor, chairs . . . you get the picture. When we were children, most of us would have been spoon-fed by adults. As we grew older, we would have learned how to feed ourselves. As adults, we are able not only to feed ourselves but also to provide for ourselves and possibly others. We go through a similar progression as we grow and mature in our faith.

When we are new Christians, we need to be spoon-fed the details of our faith. While maturing, we have to learn to feed ourselves. In today's passage, we note that mature Christians were reading the Bible daily to see for themselves what it said. They didn't want to be spoon-fed their faith by Paul any longer. Many Christians think it is their local congregation's job to feed and disciple them. When we gather together in church, there is far too much about Christian life and practice to cover in a service in addition to worship, serving the community and mission. A good church community creates space to invest in us but, ultimately, we have to take responsibility for maturing our own faith.

Is it time for you to start taking the initiative with your discipleship, so that you flourish as a follower of Jesus? To do so means finding a rhythm of learning from the Bible that works for you – for example, listening to a podcast or an online sermon in your travel time to help to build up your faith.

Psalm 1 starts by reminding us of the importance of taking personal formation seriously:

Blessed is the one
   who does not walk in step with the wicked
or stand in the way that sinners take
   or sit in the company of mockers,
but whose delight is in the law of the LORD,
   and who meditates on his law day and night.
That person is like a tree planted by streams of
     water,

which yields its fruit in season
and whose leaf does not wither –
    whatever they do prospers.
(Psalm 1.1–3)

The psalmist recognizes that someone blessed is someone who is meditating daily on the Bible. This individual
is like a thriving tree that produces fruit and its leaves do
not go brown, whatever the season. Making sure that we
are growing and maturing in our faith is central to being
someone who is healthy and emotionally well. It is also the
only way to be moulded by Jesus. If Jesus isn't shaping our
thinking and our actions, then many other things will.

YES, BUT HOW?

Starting a daily reading plan is a good way to introduce
yourself to the Bible, a little at a time. The blessed person
is the one who is meditating and chewing on God's book
and allowing it to become the foundation of life.

Use the Bible-reading guide (overleaf) to mark your
progress through the New Testament. When you have
read a chapter of each of the books in the New Testament,
tick it off. Don't just read the words; meditate on them
by asking yourself the Swedish Bible study questions (see
Day 8, p. 41). Allow the text to become a stream of living
water for your soul.

THE GOSPELS

MATTHEW ① ② ③ ④ ⑤ ⑥ ⑦ ⑧ ⑨ ⑩ ⑪ ⑫ ⑬ ⑭ ⑮ ⑯ ⑰ ⑱ ⑲ ⑳ ㉑ ㉒ ㉓ ㉔ ㉕ ㉖ ㉗ ㉘

MARK ① ② ③ ④ ⑤ ⑥ ⑦ ⑧ ⑨ ⑩ ⑪ ⑫ ⑬ ⑭ ⑮ ⑯

LUKE ① ② ③ ④ ⑤ ⑥ ⑦ ⑧ ⑨ ⑩ ⑪ ⑫ ⑬ ⑭ ⑮ ⑯ ⑰ ⑱ ⑲ ⑳ ㉑ ㉒ ㉓ ㉔

JOHN ① ② ③ ④ ⑤ ⑥ ⑦ ⑧ ⑨ ⑩ ⑪ ⑫ ⑬ ⑭ ⑮ ⑯ ⑰ ⑱ ⑲ ⑳ ㉑

ACTS ① ② ③ ④ ⑤ ⑥ ⑦ ⑧ ⑨ ⑩ ⑪ ⑫ ⑬ ⑭ ⑮ ⑯ ⑰ ⑱ ⑲ ⑳ ㉑ ㉒ ㉓ ㉔ ㉕ ㉖ ㉗ ㉘

LETTERS OF PAUL

ROMANS ① ② ③ ④ ⑤ ⑥ ⑦ ⑧ ⑨ ⑩ ⑪ ⑫ ⑬ ⑭ ⑮ ⑯

CORINTHIANS ① ② ③ ④ ⑤ ⑥ ⑦ ⑧ ⑨ ⑩ ⑪ ⑫ ⑬ ⑭ ⑮ ⑯

① ② ③ ④ ⑤ ⑥ ⑦ ⑧ ⑨ ⑩ ⑪ ⑫ ⑬

GALATIANS ① ② ③ ④ ⑤ ⑥

EPHESIANS ① ② ③ ④ ⑤ ⑥

PHILIPPIANS ① ② ③ ④

COLOSSIANS ① ② ③ ④

THESSALONIANS ① ② ③ ④ ⑤

① ② ③

TIMOTHY ① ② ③ ④ ⑤ ⑥

① ② ③ ④

TITUS ① ② ③

PHILEMON ①

LETTERS

HEBREWS ① ② ③ ④ ⑤ ⑥ ⑦ ⑧ ⑨ ⑩ ⑪ ⑫ ⑬

JAMES ① ② ③ ④ ⑤

PETER ① ② ③ ④ ⑤

① ② ③

JOHN ① ② ③ ④ ⑤

① ② ③

①

JUDE ①

PROPHECY

REVELATION ① ② ③ ④ ⑤ ⑥ ⑦ ⑧ ⑨ ⑩ ⑪ ⑫ ⑬ ⑭ ⑮ ⑯ ⑰ ⑱ ⑲ ⑳ ㉑ ㉒

TICK OFF A CHAPTER ONCE READ

DAY 27
CAN YOU SERVE LIKE JESUS?

Q. 3: How much would you say your faith leads you to serve and care for others?

> In your relationships with one another, have the same
> mindset as Christ Jesus:
>> who, being in very nature God,
>>> did not consider equality with God
>>>> something to be used to his own
>>>> advantage;
>> rather, he made himself nothing
>>> by taking the very nature of a servant,
>>> being made in human likeness.
>
> (Philippians 2.5–7)

My wife Beki and I came home from running our weekly kids' club to find that we had been burgled by someone who lived locally. We worked out who had done it but we had no real proof. This person had taken computer equipment, cameras and other items worth several thousand pounds. A few months later, we were in the local park, showing love to our neighbours by handing out free burgers and drinks, when who should come by for his free burger? None other than our friendly neighbourhood burglar.

I wonder why we do kind things? Do we do them to be completely selfless or do we do them to appear to be generous and caring? It is very hard for us to do everything without motives. Real generosity, however, requires us to move away from doing something to be seen and noticed. Jesus speaks about this so beautifully in Matthew 6.2:

> So when you give to the needy, do not announce it with trumpets, as the hypocrites do in the synagogues and on the streets, to be honoured by others. Truly I tell you, they have received their reward in full.

When I read the part about 'announcing with trumpets', it reminds me of those charity events when someone hands over money with one of those large charity cheques. Time and time again, Jesus healed people and sent them away, saying they were to tell no one that he'd done it. His asking for discretion was partly due to his desire to delay his arrest, trial and crucifixion, but it was also because it was in his nature, as described in Philippians 2.

In today's passage, Paul teaches the early Christian church in Philippi how to be united and love one another by pointing them to the example of Jesus, the God who became man. In his humanity, Jesus showed us God's character and demonstrated humility, in being willing to give up his rights in order to obey God and serve people. Paul emphasizes that if we say we follow Jesus, we should try to do likewise, by serving out of love for God and others. While Jesus was recognized as a rabbi, he spent much of his time with ordinary people, and most often with outcasts. Jesus was generous with his time, sitting and eating with those who were rejected and to whom other rabbis would never have given time.

We have a choice about our attitudes towards situations and people that we encounter. It is easy to live life motivated by pride ('I'll do this kind thing so that people think I'm great') or selfishness ('Why can't I do/have exactly what I want?'). But Paul wants us to look to Jesus as an example of countercultural living. In the preceding verses, Paul encourages the Philippians to put one another's needs first because, ultimately, it will lead to unity. If I consider you above me and you consider me above you, then a beautiful thing happens: we have a community in which everyone is respected and no one is despised. The nature of Jesus, described in Philippians 2, is the very nature we are invited to share and be shaped by.

So, what happened to the burglar and his burger? He came by and we handed him his burger with love. We wanted to withhold it from him, we wanted to say something, but none of that would have come from Jesus.

YES, BUT HOW?

Aim today to do something that serves another person, but in such a way that he or she is unlikely to notice or thank you. It can be a lot of fun.

As you reflect, you might like to listen to one of the following songs, which can be found online:

- Hillsong's 'This is our God' reminds us that our God came to serve.
- Graham Kendrick's 'Servant King', if you'd like a 1980s throwback.

PRAYER

Christ has no body now but yours.
No hands, no feet on earth but yours.
Yours are the eyes through which he looks
      compassion on this world.
Yours are the feet with which he walks to do good.
Yours are the hands through which he blesses all the
      world.
Yours are the hands, yours are the feet, yours are the
      eyes,
you are his body.
Christ has no body now on earth but yours.
Amen.
(Teresa of Avila, 1515–1582)

DAY 28
CHANGING YOUR HABITS TO LIVE IN SYNC WITH CREATION

Q. 7: How much are your daily habits changing to reflect God's care for his creation?

Where were you when I laid the earth's foundation?
  Tell me, if you understand.
Who marked off its dimensions? Surely you know!
  Who stretched a measuring line across it?
On what were its footings set,
  or who laid its cornerstone –
while the morning stars sang together
  and all the angels shouted for joy?

Who shut up the sea behind doors
  when it burst forth from the womb,
when I made the clouds its garment
  and wrapped it in thick darkness,
when I fixed limits for it
  and set its doors and bars in place,
when I said, 'This far you may come and no farther;
  here is where your proud waves halt'?

Have you ever given orders to the morning,
  or shown the dawn its place . . . ?
(Job 38.4–13)

It can be so easy to go about our day not lifting our thoughts above what we see.

The worst thing for me is commuting; it's so busy that, in the heat of the moment, I lose sight of the beauty around me. I often cycle past Buckingham Palace; when I stop at the traffic lights, I stare at those, rather than admire the building, to make sure that I don't lose a second! However, this passage from Job forcefully reminds me of the glory of the universe, and God's sovereignty over it. Even a sunset over east London's imperfect skyline of tower blocks brings wonder and removes self-centredness. I think of the depths of the 'earth's foundation' or the power of the ocean's 'proud waves' and I am humbled. Like Job in a later chapter, I quietly whisper, 'I am unworthy.' But the good news of the gospel is that we are not the centre of the universe – it's much bigger and more beautiful than that – and the one who is its centre thinks us worthy to be noticed, to be redeemed at great price, and to serve as his hands and feet.

God has given us responsibility to steward the earth: to preserve its beauty, lessen suffering and demonstrate God's care to others. It's hard to know how, personally, we can each help the environment. However, I believe that, by making a habit of building on small, even seemingly insignificant actions, we can work towards a noble purpose, which cultivates a humble and grateful spirit within us.

The gospel starts with God creating the world and placing humankind in a perfect garden to tend it and care for it (Genesis 2.15). The first command was to partner with God in caring for the plants. When Jesus died for us he did it to free us from sin and to restore us to our original partnership with God. The story of the gospel is not only a story of salvation but also one of partnership to tend to and care for creation.

YES, BUT HOW?

QUESTIONS TO CONSIDER

Think about your daily life.

- What can you change to lessen your impact on the environment?
- Can you declare that there's something more important than convenience and comfort for you and those around you?
- What's your carbon footprint? Do you know what impact your life is having on the planet? Why not take the carbon footprint test to find out (at: <www.carbon footprint.com/calculator.aspx>)?
- **Can you travel responsibly?** Can you find a more sustainable way of travelling today – for example, using a car share, cycling, walking or taking the bus?
- **Can you reduce your waste?** Can you make a change that uses less plastic or no plastic?
- **Can you eat sustainably?** Food production is a major driver of wildlife extinction. What we eat contributes to around a quarter of global greenhouse gas emissions and is responsible for almost 60 per cent of global biodiversity loss. Can you make a commitment to eat less meat or to shop locally for locally produced products?

DAY 29
WHAT WOULD JESUS TWEET?

Q. 17: How much time do you regularly spend engaging with the Bible?

Q. 8: How much does tragedy and injustice in the world move you to action?

> Is not this the kind of fasting I have chosen:
> to loose the chains of injustice
>   and untie the cords of the yoke,
> to set the oppressed free
>   and break every yoke?
> Is it not to share your food with the hungry
>   and to provide the poor wanderer with shelter –
> when you see the naked, to clothe them,
>   and not to turn away from your own flesh and blood?
> (Isaiah 58.6–7)

As far as I know, Jesus never signed an online petition, retweeted a news article or shared a social media meme to show that he 'really had read it and cared enough'. I mean, obviously, Jesus didn't do any of those things; my point is that he didn't react to tragedy and injustice by picking a response that looked good, and possibly felt good, but in reality didn't do a lot.

What Jesus did do was move into the neighbourhood. He hung out with people on the edges, speaking with and touching those branded by the 'tabloids' of the time as benefit cheats, liars, thieves – those usually blamed for all society's problems. He didn't associate with them for just an afternoon either. Instead, he gave them three years of ministry – and his life.

The challenge for us on this journey of discipleship is to be moved to action beyond a social-media post that's forgotten in a week. Jesus calls us to be moved in our very gut, to feel as if we have no other choice but to give the best of our years to make a difference, face to face, hand to hand, with and alongside others.

There are so many tragedies and injustices – we can't give ourselves to engaging with all of them. But we can think and pray about whether there is something that does hit us in the gut like nothing else. Maybe it's to do with the refugee crisis, homelessness, gender equality or climate change.

I heard about the work of a Christian charity called Open Doors 15 years ago. As I learned of the persecution of Christians all over the world, I had to ask myself, 'Am I willing to allow these stories to break me or will I step back and approach them in a way that doesn't change me?' I realized that, from hearing about tragedy in the past, I had created a defence mechanism that stopped me from being moved. My response was simply to pray, 'Holy Spirit break my heart for what breaks my Father's heart.' Since then, I have visited a number of places. I've spent time in Ebola treatment centres in Liberia and with Christians on the Syria–Lebanon border. When we ask God to break our hearts, we have to back up the request with a willingness to be broken, to be proactive and to start to do something about injustice.

When God breaks our hearts, he gives us each a different type of heartbreak. For some, it's for the poor in a local neighbourhood; for others, it's domestic violence; for yet others, it's the environment, and so on. Having a specific heartbreak doesn't mean that we shouldn't care about all the other problems, but when God breaks our hearts over one issue, we become very passionate about that thing. A broken heart must then lead to action of some kind. The cost will look different for each of us – but there is a cost.

How do we find out what God is breaking our hearts for? The more time we spend with God, the more we will understand what the heartbreak is for.

WHAT IF I JUST DON'T KNOW, AND I DON'T FEEL HEARTBROKEN ABOUT ANYTHING?

Start by confessing and asking if there is a spiritual blockage in your life. Is there something stopping you from allowing your heart to engage with God's? Sometimes our own protection mechanisms stop God from changing us. For example, if we have been hurt in the past, we might hold God at arm's length.

We can also start by helping someone else with their great heartbreak. For example, we can join a group passionate about caring for the environment, tackling child poverty or addressing a local injustice.

YES, BUT HOW?

1 Ditch the click-and-share on social media, unless you think it really will make a difference.

2 Take time to think about what tragedy or injustice is hitting you in the gut. Research the issue, explore the first steps necessary to become involved.

3 Pray for guidance about taking a small step to make a difference. Reach out to others who are passionate about a similar issue or topic and ask to join them.

4 And then do it! Who knows what might happen?

PRAYER

The Spirit of the Lord is on me,
because you are anointing me
to proclaim good news to the poor,
to proclaim freedom for the prisoners
and recovery of sight for the blind;
to set the oppressed free
and to proclaim the year of the Lord's favour.
Amen.
(Based on Isaiah 61.1–2 and Luke 4.18–19)

JESUS PREPARES OUR FEET FOR NEW WAYS OF WALKING

Q. 14: How much of an impact do your beliefs and the Bible have on your attitude towards culture, the world and your community?

You call me 'Teacher' and 'Lord', and rightly so, for that is what I am. Now that I, your Lord and Teacher, have washed your feet, you also should wash one another's feet.
(John 13.13–14)

When the Millennium Bridge, pedestrian crossing over the Thames, was first opened in 2000, it mysteriously began falling apart. Despite excellent work by the best engineers, screws were working loose and no one knew why – until the engineers discovered something surprising. The original designers had calculated the weight of people, footfall, extra load and more. However, they hadn't realized that, when the bridge was busy, people would begin to walk in step with one another. This mass synchronization resulted in resonance – waves were created along the bridge, causing the bridge to wobble and all the screws to work loose.

The world we live in is constantly pushing us to conform, to walk 'in sync' with it. We have power over our own choices but we don't have power over the choices others make or the patterns by which whole communities live.

But people's choices and patterns of community behaviour are powerful. Sometimes, we don't even know that we are conforming to these destructive ways. Like walking over the Millennium Bridge in a crowd, we don't realize that we're walking in sync with the world.

Recently, we had a food delivery at the church and I chatted to the delivery guy. He had been born in east London, into what was very much an east London family. When he suggested to his family that he'd prefer not to leave school and go to college, he was told, 'We don't do that in this family. You're going to work with your uncle.' When he'd go out for a drink with them and then decide to leave early, he was asked, 'What's wrong with you? Get another one down your neck!' When he fell in love with a girl from India, they said, 'What do you think is wrong with people from east London? You're not marrying her!' His early life was about being told that he couldn't diverge from 'what we do around here'. If he tried to do anything differently, he was seen as challenging the norm. Today, he regrets working for a criminal uncle who let him go to jail; he regrets staying for one more drink and having to fight to recover from alcoholism for 20 years; and he regrets not marrying the woman he wanted to marry. His is a life not only of regret but also of conformity.

Jesus washed away the disciples' desire to walk in sync with the world; he prepared their feet for a new way of walking – his way. He came to serve, to act justly, to love mercy, to walk humbly (Micah 6.8), to seek and save the lost (Luke 19.10), teaching them not to conform (Romans 12.2). Do your feet need washing? Is God calling you to wash the feet of others? Jesus wants to prepare our feet for new, beautiful ways of walking that show the true pattern with which the whole of creation yearns to be in sync – that found in the life of the Father, Son and Holy Spirit.

YES, BUT HOW?

1 **Ask** God to show you the wrong ways in which you are conforming to the world – any bad patterns that you are following and choices that are habitually destructive.

2 **Wait** in silence and listen, perhaps set a timer to 1, 2 or 5 minutes, if it helps, and see what God says or prompts you to do.

3 **Write** down or draw what you think the Holy Spirit said. You might write a paragraph or a list.

4 **Act** tell someone what you want to do or leave behind. He or she can hold you to account, helping you to act on what you have heard and, as a result, live differently.

DAY 31
TAKING TIME TO CELEBRATE

Q. 5: How willing are you to put in place helpful boundaries?

The Israelites are to observe the Sabbath, celebrating it for the generations to come as a lasting covenant.
(Exodus 31.16)

> The Sabbath is the presence of God in the world, open to the soul of man. God is not in things of space, but in moments of time . . . Shabbat (Sabbath) comes with its own holiness; we enter not simply a day, but an atmosphere.
> (Abraham Joshua Heschel, *The Sabbath* (Macmillan, 2005), p. 16)

On the Sabbath, we pause to remind ourselves that we aren't God; that we are human beings, not human 'doings'; and that we aren't the Saviour. Hitting pause and taking stock of life is the healthiest thing we can do. When we pause and spend time appreciating all that we have, we nurture gratitude.

Hard-wired into the Jewish people is a rhythm of stopping and celebrating the moments that are significant to them as God's people, often annually. Passover, Yom Kippur (the Day of Atonement), Sukkot (the Feast of Tabernacles),

Hanukkah (the Festival of Lights), Rosh Hashanah (the Jewish New Year) and others are all moments when they celebrate God's work in their lives. Each of these occasions was designed to remind the Jewish people of all that God had given them and done for them.

Sadly, for many, the Christian festivals of Christmas and Easter are caught up with food, sweets, drinks, chocolate and expensive gift giving. We have somewhat lost the beauty and wonder of celebrating.

Celebrating itself is very healthy and even godly. God wants us to celebrate – the parties in the Bible usually lasted for a week! Celebrating isn't about getting drunk or spending a lot of money – it's about thanking God for the good things that he has given us and being happy for great moments. It's about pausing and enjoying what there is. The Bible tells us that God took a day of rest after creating the world, when he enjoyed what he had created. He hit pause and celebrated.

It is healthy and godly to click pause and celebrate, daily, weekly and beyond.

When you sit down exhausted, having finally put all the children to bed, celebrate the fact that you managed to get through the day. Instead of trying to switch off by watching TV or scrolling through social media, why not take a moment – maybe with a cup of tea – to thank God for the great chat you had with a friend and for God's guidance throughout the day. Pause, thank God and say 'well done' to yourself.

When you come home from work, celebrate the work you've completed today. Enjoy remembering that wonderful moment when the whole team was laughing, and think gratefully of the lunch break when the sun was shining on your face. Take a moment to thank God for those experiences, saying 'well done' to yourself and resting.

Taking time for Sabbath rest involves taking time to celebrate. It is about slowing down, looking back and enjoying what was good. Each week we are commanded by God to hit pause and allow ourselves to savour and celebrate the week that is now behind us, and all the ways that God has made himself known and shown his goodness to us.

A BOOK

One of the most profound and helpful books I have ever read on the Sabbath is *The Sabbath* by Rabbi Abraham Joshua Heschel. If you want to develop your understanding of the Sabbath, it's worth a look.

YES, BUT HOW?

Click pause and celebrate every day! You might want to put an alarm on your phone to remind yourself to celebrate each day. A good friend of mine sets an alarm at 5.25 p.m., not as a reminder that he finishes work at 5.30 p.m. but to give him a moment, just before the work day ends, to thank God for it and for what he has achieved, and to hand to God what he didn't manage to do. In this short moment, he appreciates the opportunity to work and thanks God for the strength to do so.

Next time you post a picture on social media, why don't you put #celebratedmydayandmyGod by it as a way of appreciating how you've spent your day?

Take a day off every week to celebrate all the good moments you've had and to celebrate God's provision. Taking a day off demonstrates our trust in God's provision instead of in our own works.

DAY 32
NOT AN INDIVIDUAL EVENT

Q. 6: To what extent are you serving Jesus in collaboration with others?

So Barnabas went to Tarsus to look for Saul, and when he had found him, he brought him to Antioch. For a whole year they met with the church and taught a great many people. And in Antioch the disciples were first called Christians. (Acts 11.25–26 ESV)

Have you ever watched the hundred-metre sprint in the Olympics? Before the race starts, the athletes are so completely focused on their goal that each of them might as well be running completely alone. They avoid engaging with anyone who might distract them from their aim to run the quickest race they can.

Do we sometimes bring this attitude into church? Have you ever heard it said, 'Just forget about everyone else and focus on Jesus'? Devotion and commitment to Jesus is wonderful and so important, but our spiritual life isn't a competitive hundred-metre sprint in which all that matters is doing the best we can. We are also called to look out for, encourage and enable one another.

In this passage, Barnabas really shows us what that means. Things were going well for him in Antioch – he had built a reputation on being an amazing servant of God. But he remembered an old friend called Saul (see Acts 9.27), someone whom he believed God had great plans for. He *took time out*, *journeyed to find* Saul (Antioch to Tarsus and back was approximately a 250-mile trip), brought him back to work with him, and *encouraged* him to follow the path to which God had called him.

After being encouraged and supported by Barnabas, Saul (whom we know as Paul) set off to spread the message of Jesus around the known world and also wrote a large part of the New Testament. The impact that Barnabas had by believing in him and making sacrifices to help him to flourish cannot be understated.

Jesus calls us into community, not only to run as quickly as we personally can but also to look around to see whom we can help and raise up, whom we can support and inspire. You are not alone and your faith is not only your own; you are part of the family of God. God saved you so that your story, your experiences, can help someone else.

On Day 18, I told the story of a man who was struggling with prescription drugs. The issue the man had could have been anything – a family death, money trouble, problems with a teenage child or employment difficulties. The important thing was that he was trapped in a deep hole and unable to get out. A lawyer walked past and heard the man's cry for help. The lawyer was concerned for the guy. He said, 'I'll make some calls; I'll send a few emails; I will see what I can do.' Before he walked away, he dropped a business card into the hole.

Next, a priest passed by and heard the man's cry for help. 'I will say a prayer for you, brother,' he said and walked on.

The third person to walk past is you. You are the third person in the story. A little like the story of the good

Samaritan, you now have a question to ask. Do you behave like the lawyer and send a few emails? Do you offer to pray like the priest or do you jump into the hole? How willing are you to be the solution that Jesus saved you to be?

YES, BUT HOW?

Who is your Saul? Someone who you can see doing what you do but going further in the future?	Whom can you be an encouragement to today?	Whom can you share wisdom with this week?	Who are the people you know you need to give more time and attention to, to help them on their path?

PRAYER

Help me to see something in others, as others see
    something in me.
Lead me to invest in those who are stuck,
    give support to those who need a lift
    and give encouragement to those who are confused.
Like Barnabas, help me to look for, and draw alongside,
    those in whose lives you want me to play a part.
Today, help me to keep my eyes open for those in whose
    lives I can make a difference.
Amen.

DAY 33
GOD KNOWS YOU

Q. 12: To what extent is your relationship with God being regularly cultivated and deepened?

For you created my inmost being.
(Psalm 139.13)

We long to be fully known. We want people to know us and to like what they see. But this natural, God-given desire can be twisted in our culture. Posting pictures of ourselves online to share our experiences can turn into running after 'likes' and affection. And then we can become insecure if people don't 'like' what they see.

My son has a social-media account for his hamster. On it, he posts pictures of his hamster climbing the stairs, hunting for food, having a cuddle and wearing a miniature woolly hat. This account now has more followers than his own personal social-media account. The hamster is more 'liked' than he and I are put together. Imagine how that makes me feel!

This psalm of David's celebrates the fact that God created our 'inmost being', the core of who we are. When God looks at us, he likes what he sees. God knows and celebrates us. He designed us, knows us by name and loves every part of us. Sometimes we forget that and chase after love, affection and appreciation in all the wrong places.

When I was a youth worker, preparing a course that I was to run called 'I have a teenager, get me out of here!', I read a parenting book. There was one chapter that really struck me and sticks with me today, particularly now that my two children are teenagers. It said that if parents don't hug their teenagers many times a day, then the teenagers will look for touch and attention in other places. It advised that parents could slow down the dating game for many young people by showing them attention and affection at home.

In John 14.7, Jesus says 'If you really know me, you will know my Father as well. From now on, you do know him and have seen him.' The heart of the gospel is that you can know God and that you are known by him.

Are there any parts of your 'inmost being' with which you are currently struggling? Maybe certain desires are confusing you or you hate part of your body? Maybe you've never even realized God loves every part of you, and that it is therefore right to love yourself.

Being honest and talking to God about your struggles is a good first step. He will never be shocked by anything you say to him in prayer. Second, you can talk to other people in God's family. These might be Christians in church whom you trust and respect.

Imagine what life would be like if we were to live every day remembering that we are championed by God. What would our prayers sound like if we realized how well God knows us and how deeply he loves us?

YES, BUT HOW?

Why not try one or more of the following activities today?

- **Read** Psalm 139 aloud to yourself.

- **Write** bits of it on sticky notes and put them somewhere you can see them.
- **Celebrate** your body through exercise, dance or some other appropriate way.
- **Renew** your mind by naming anything that is stopping you from loving yourself the way God loves you – talk to a trusted friend about it.
- **Be creative** and try putting this psalm to music or using a different art form to bring it to life.

HOW MUCH DO TRAGEDY AND INJUSTICE MOVE YOU TO TAKE ACTION?

Q. 8: How much do tragedy and injustice in the world move you to action?

The poor and needy search for water,
but there is none;
their tongues are parched with thirst.
But I the LORD will answer them;
I, the God of Israel, will not forsake them.
I will make rivers flow on barren heights,
and springs within the valleys.
I will turn the desert into pools of water,
and the parched ground into springs.
(Isaiah 41.17–18)

The greatest tragedy in the world today is not injustice but, rather, the failure of all people, particularly Christians, to rise up against injustice. The Way of Jesus is to side with the poor, the marginalized and the ignored. However, those who follow the Way of Jesus can often overlook this very issue. Have you ever heard someone say, 'Why does God allow suffering?' Jesus left the members of the Church as the administrators of his kingdom, so the question should therefore be 'Why do Christians allow suffering, tragedy and injustice?'

As Jesus increases his grip on our lives, we should find that we have a better grasp of what's happening around us. Without Jesus, we can fall into the trap of being so self-absorbed that we miss what is happening beyond ourselves. As we allow Jesus to shape what we think, how we feel and what we notice, we should start to see injustice in the world without passively accepting it. It's too easy to 'turn a blind eye' when we are meant to look and to act on what we see.

God sees the needy and he promises to respond to their thirst. Are you willing to do the same? Are you willing to open your eyes to see injustice, need and problems? Are you willing to be the answer, whenever possible, to the problem?

Jesus started his ministry by setting out a manifesto for his work. In the synagogue in Nazareth, Jesus read directly from Isaiah 61, which makes it clear that those who are filled with the Spirit are also people who are anointed to carry out his work with the poor and those experiencing tragedy.

The Spirit of the Lord is on me,
　　because he has anointed me
　　to *proclaim good news* to the poor.
He has sent me to *proclaim freedom* for the
　　　prisoners
　　and *recovery of sight* for the blind,
to set the *oppressed free*,
　　to proclaim the *year of the Lord's favour*.
(Luke 4.18–19, emphasis added)

The Holy Spirit had anointed Jesus to speak the gospel, proclaim freedom to the imprisoned, healing and forgiveness, and the Spirit wants to do the same through us.

YES, BUT HOW?

Increasing your awareness of injustice is about becoming more aware of the world around you. Take some simple steps to try to understand what is going on. Sometimes it's as simple as looking beyond your own bubble. If you don't read or watch the news, it is very easy to be unaware of what is happening in the world.

Step one

Watch the news or read a news website; pray for what you see and hear. Reading the BBC News website can give you lots of material for prayer and for action.

Step two

Spend time visiting <www.tearfund.org> and <www. christianaid.org.uk> to investigate what is happening in the world and to see what needs there are. Sign up for the Open Doors monthly prayer letter (at: <www.opendoorsuk. org> to receive specific information about persecution globally, so that you can respond in prayer.

Step three

Pray 'break my heart for what breaks yours'. If you're willing, make this a daily prayer, inviting God to increase your awareness. Ask for help to find one simple thing that you can change to make a difference, such as buying fair-trade goods, writing to an MP or going on a protest rally.

QUESTION TO CONSIDER

What can you do today to make a difference in the life of someone that you, until this point, may have overlooked?

WORSHIP RESPONSE

Hillsong United produced a track called 'Hosanna'. Download it or find it online, and spend some time listening to the lyrics. Use them to pray for God to open your eyes to the things that you've overlooked every day, and for your heart to be broken for the things that break God's.

YOUR HANDS ARE HIS HANDS: DO WHAT JESUS DID

Q. 3: How much would you say your faith leads you to serve and care for others?

When Jesus came down from the mountainside, large crowds followed him. A man with leprosy came and knelt before him and said, 'Lord, if you are willing, you can make me clean.'

Jesus reached out his hand and touched the man. 'I am willing,' he said. 'Be clean!' Immediately he was cleansed of his leprosy. Then Jesus said to him, 'See that you don't tell anyone. But go, show yourself to the priest and offer the gift Moses commanded, as a testimony to them.
(Matthew 8.1–4)

In 2001, James, a 25-year-old builder, crushed his hand in an accident on a building site. The injury damaged his bones, tendons and nerves. After extensive surgery, his hand looked fine but he was unable to move it, clench his fist or point. James was told that if he didn't use his hand, it would never move. However, if he was willing to start using it, moving it a little each day, then it might gain strength and function. As he wasn't able to work, he volunteered at a local food bank. He helped to stack shelves and pack bags. As time went on, the more he used his hand to serve those in need, the more his hand started to function properly – gripping, holding and handing over bags of food. I wonder how your hands function? Have they been used to serve others lately? Are they stiff or are they flexible?

We are disciples of Rabbi Jesus; he is the one we want to be like today. In today's passage, we first need to understand that the only thing considered filthier than contact with a leper was contact with a dead body. Here, Jesus had come down from teaching on the mountainside when a man with leprosy (an incurable disease in the ancient world) knelt before him to ask whether he would be willing to make him clean. The leper did not doubt Jesus' power or ability to heal him; he only questioned whether Jesus would be willing to do so. Jesus responds by reaching out and touching him. Imagine what those looking on would have thought of this? Jesus didn't have to touch the leper in order to heal him, he could have simply spoken a word. But how much more meaningful was it that Jesus was prepared to use his hands?

In the past, when I was working in situations that felt pretty hopeless and overwhelming, I kept a David Orr quote in my work diary that said, 'Hope is a verb with its sleeves rolled up' (from *Hope Is Imperative* (Island Press), p. 54). Sometimes I think we need to show God that we are ready and willing to be used by him, by putting our hands in situations that feel unclean, uncomfortable or unpleasant, even when it takes a while for our hearts and minds to catch up.

Just before Christmas, I often take a couple of days to retreat to gain some perspective on the season and to avoid rushing through Advent. One year, it had been a really good autumn, so I decided to use my retreat time differently. For three days, rather than going to a quiet retreat centre, I went to a shelter for the homeless in Watford. I helped to cook soup, feed the homeless and played lots of cards. It was a great experience, but something hap-pened one day that required my hands to serve while my head and heart were still unwilling and lagging behind. A heroin addict came in; his clothes were dropping off him and his shoes were soaking wet. He stank, his breath and teeth were awful, and all I wanted to do was gag. My head said, 'He's an addict with self-inflicted problems', and my heart didn't want to engage. But my hands were ready. We stripped him, clothed him and fed him. My main memory was of putting new shoes on his half-rotten, never-washed feet. Sometimes your hands have to act before your heart and head catch up. It's only then that your heart can be-come like that of Jesus.

YES, BUT HOW?

QUESTIONS TO CONSIDER

Whom do you identify with in this passage?

- The leper, broken, rejected and unclean, asking God if he is really willing to heal you, make you clean and have a relationship with you?
- To you, Jesus says that he is willing.
- The disciples or the people in the crowd?
- To you, Jesus says that he has given you the same power (Romans 8.11; Ephesians 1.19) and that, if you're willing, he is more than willing to use you in his kingdom.

REFLECTION

To help you to reflect further, take a moment to listen to a song by Tim Hughes called 'May the words of my mouth', which can easily be found online (it's an oldie, but a goodie).

Who is your leper?

Write in the outline below whom you struggle to touch. It might not be someone with a disease; it might be someone you don't get along with.

PRAYER

Hold out your hands in front of you and pray this very simple prayer from the Psalms. Repeat it a few times to allow it to sink in.

I call to you, LORD, every day;
    I spread out my hands to you.
(Psalm 88.9)

DAY 36
JESUS CAN'T BE A HOBBY

Q. 12: To what extent is your relationship with God being regularly cultivated and deepened?

The night before Jesus was crucified, he had dinner with his disciples, who had followed him for three years. As you read the passage, note the different titles Jesus was given.

When evening came, Jesus was reclining at the table with the Twelve. And while they were eating, he said, 'Truly I tell you, one of you will betray me.'

They were very sad and began to say to him one after the other, 'Surely you don't mean me, *Lord*?'

Jesus replied, 'The one who has dipped his hand into the bowl with me will betray me. The Son of Man will go just as it is written about him. But woe to that man who betrays the Son of Man! It would be better for him if he had not been born.'

Then Judas, the one who would betray him, said, 'Surely you don't mean me, *Rabbi*?'
(Matthew 26.20–25, emphasis added)

The Greek word for 'Lord' is *kurios*, which means 'one who holds absolute ownership and rulership' and is a term of worship. The Greek word for 'rabbi' is *rhabbi*, which means a person who is recognized by the Jewish people as a teacher of the faith.

What do you call Jesus? Is Jesus the Lord of your life or a moral teacher for your life? One receives full control and worship, while the other is given the position of teacher and instructor. Jesus wants to be the Lord of our lives and not just the teacher. Judas strayed because he respected Jesus but didn't give Jesus the worship of his heart. Judas wanted Jesus' teaching but not his authority . . . What about you?

Many of us have a hobby. Hobbies are what we do in our spare time; we spend our spare money on our hobbies and they're relaxing. Hobbies are done in 'spare' time, with 'spare' resources and with 'spare' energy. There is a huge danger that we might treat Jesus like that. For some people, Jesus' command to follow him seems to be taken as little more than a spiritual hobby, based on a decision to accept Jesus. In such cases, faith in him is an occasional weekend pastime, provided it doesn't conflict with other interests or cost us anything.

There are different kinds of faith.

- **Hobby faith** Practised in your spare time with your spare resources. Jesus is someone you enjoy but don't commit to.
- **Private faith** Faith kept to yourself and practised in private. Jesus is your private friend.
- **Moral faith** A belief that faith in God will bring you happiness, and that a good, moral life will help you to find your purpose. Jesus is a morality teacher.
- **'Die to' faith** Jesus describes this as 'dying to self'; in other words, your life changes significantly because you hand it over to the Way of Jesus.

Questions to consider

It is worth asking a few questions to diagnose if Jesus is a hobby or a primary part of your life.

- Do you give financially to Jesus' mission from the first portion of your income or do you give from what is left at the end?
- Do you worship with others weekly or do you worship with others when you have nothing else on? Is church a priority or is it set aside when something else is happening?
- Does your faith shape your choices about how you spend your time or do you tend to be led by how you feel?

It is claimed that the missionary and theologian E. Stanley Jones once said, 'Jesus is Lord of all or he is not Lord at all.' Ask yourself where Jesus fits in your life. Is it possible that you have made Jesus a hobby, someone to engage with in your spare time? Jesus did not die to be a religious hobby, but to save you from your own destructive ways. Judas loved spending time with Jesus; he listened to his teaching and followed him. But, in the end, what truly mattered was that Judas was unable to give Jesus his heart.

YES, BUT HOW?

How do you approach Jesus? Is he your Lord? Do you acknowledge and submit to his absolute authority in your life or do you prefer to see him as a teacher? Jesus does not want to be with you only when you have time; he wants to be with you every moment of your day.

There are many things in life that clamour for our undivided attention, that want to 'lord' it over us. The Roman

Empire, 2,000 years ago, created a culture in which everyone had to say 'Caesar is lord' many times during the day. People would say it when greeting one another and when sales were made. The early Church adopted this custom but, instead, its members would say to one another 'Jesus is Lord'.

SET A THREE-HOUR ALARM

On your phone or watch, set an alarm to beep every three hours. In that moment, whatever you are doing, say to yourself 'Jesus is Lord'. If you allow it to, continually reminding yourself of who Jesus is will become an ingrained rhythm of surrender.

DAY 37
REPRESENTING JESUS

Q. 20: To what extent does your reading of the Bible point you towards Jesus and how to live for him?

All this is from God, who reconciled us to himself through Christ and gave us the ministry of reconciliation: that God was reconciling the world to himself in Christ, not counting people's sins against them. And he has committed to us the message of reconciliation. We are therefore Christ's ambassadors, as though God were making his appeal through us. We implore you on Christ's behalf: be reconciled to God. (2 Corinthians 5.18–20)

The TV show *The West Wing* not only taught me so much about life in the White House – the politics and culture – but it also highlighted how US writers caricatured foreign ambassadors. None was more comical than the UK Ambassador, Lord Marbury. This character would appear in the odd episode, with his upper-class English accent and love for tea with a shot of whisky, and talk about the Queen as if she were a close personal friend.

What I also learned was that ambassadors are representatives of their native countries in foreign lands. They actively promote their people's interests and values to other countries. For each ambassador, this, of course, means living in another nation for an extended period, engaging with its people and, if necessary, learning its language(s). Paul uses the ambassadorial motif of promoting interests and values when talking about believers and their daily lives.

So, what does it mean to be Christ's ambassadors?

It means that we are sent out. We are permanent representatives of another kingdom while living in this world. Christ doesn't command us to hide away from the world and to avoid engaging with it; neither does he tell us to assimilate completely. We are of God's kingdom, living in a worldly kingdom. We are ambassadors of King Jesus while serving in the kingdom of humanity. As representatives of Christ in the world, we are to demonstrate his values to those around us.

As ambassadors of King Jesus, we are told in today's passage that we have been given a ministry of reconciliation (or 'reconnection'). We are not to be ambassadors who sit in our residences and preach from a distance. No! We are to be ambassadors who get our hands dirty. We are to go out and meet the people, to demonstrate our kingdom values to those around us. King Jesus commissions us to go out and to be his hands, his mouth and his ears to a broken, hurting and lost world.

YES, BUT HOW?

The task of being King Jesus' ambassadors to the world does look and sound a little terrifying. But you can start with small steps. Ask yourself today whether there is one person you can show love to; someone who needs to hear today that God loves them. Jesus' kingdom values are radical; they are attractive and, as we to try to demonstrate them (while being aware of our failings and God's immeasurable grace), people will be drawn to our message.

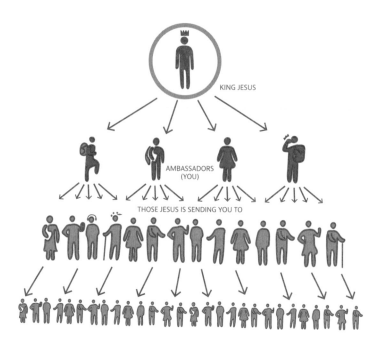

KING JESUS

AMBASSADORS
(YOU)

THOSE JESUS IS SENDING YOU TO

Jesus is King and he is sending you out, like many before you, to be an ambassador to others.

QUESTIONS TO CONSIDER

- To whom is Jesus sending you to be an ambassador today, this week or this month?
- What do you need to do differently to be an effective ambassador?

YOU ARE NOT A BEGGAR

Q. 9: How engaged are you in a personal and community prayer life?

[Jesus said,] 'And I will do whatever you ask in my name, so that the Father [God] may be glorified in the Son [Jesus]. You may ask me for anything in my name, and I will do it.' (John 14.13–14)

It doesn't take much to notice that we live in a society that is riddled with fear. We are fearful of health issues, fearful of money troubles, fearful of the future, fearful of politics, and so on and so forth. Our society might be gripped and driven by fear but fear isn't God's desire for us. Prayer is the antidote to fear because it acknowledges the one who has the real power.

> Faith and prayer are invisible things, but they
>   make impossible things possible.
> It is God's job to work the wonders . . .
> Our part is the simplest: to pray, believe and wait!

A friend gave me a note some time ago. It read:

Don't just pray about what seems logical + ~~possible~~. Pray HARD about the '~~impossible~~' → God will show you that NOTHING, nothing, nothing, nothing is impossible with him. Ever. Period. End of story!

Matthew 19.26 is a beautiful reminder of this: 'Jesus looked at them and said, "With man this is impossible, but with God all things are possible."'

There is such potential in prayer, if only we would see it. Many of us don't have a prayer issue; we have an identity issue. How we see ourselves affects how we understand the activity of prayer. If we see ourselves as beggars who have slipped into the throne room of God, we will approach the King, grovelling for help. But if we see ourselves as adopted sons or daughters who have been given authority to carry out God's business on earth, as ambassadors of the nation of Jesus, then we will approach with a very different posture. We aren't beggars; we belong to *the* royal family.

As you walk today, do so not as a beggar but as royalty. Romans 8.14–15 says (emphasis added):

For those who are led by the Spirit of God are the children of God. The Spirit you received does not make

YOU ARE NOT A BEGGAR

you slaves [beggars], so that you live in *fear* again; rather, the Spirit you received brought about your *adoption* to sonship. And by him we cry, 'Abba, Father.'

Which means when we pray, we do so with authority, not fear.

Brother Andrew, a missionary from the Netherlands who travelled the world smuggling Bibles into remote countries, writes:

There are no borders, no prison walls, no doors that are closed when we pray. The political, economic, military and spiritual leaders of the world may not know our names, but we can have more influence on their plans than all of their closest advisers put together. While many things may seem impossible from a human standpoint, in the realm of prayer there are no impossibilities.
(*Prayer: The real battle* (Open Doors, 2010), p. 9)

YES, BUT HOW?

Find a pen and some paper, and write down two things you would like to pray for every day this week, such as

- a **situation** in your life you would love to see changed;
- a **person** who is on your heart;
- a **miracle** that is in the realms of impossibility in your own life.

Choose a *regular time* to pray. While eating breakfast, making a cup of tea or in bed before you go to sleep. You can change your prayer points after a while, if you like.

DAY 39
WITH US OR AGAINST US?

Q. 16: To what extent are you allowing yourself to learn from those who think differently from you?

John said to him, 'Teacher, we saw someone casting out demons in your name, and we tried to stop him, because he was not following us.' But Jesus said, 'Do not stop him, for no one who does a mighty work in my name will be able soon afterwards to speak evil of me. For the one who is not against us is for us.
(Mark 9.38–40 ESV)

This passage reflects how we sometimes speak to one another: 'You say you're following Jesus but . . .'; 'If you were a real Christian, you would . . .' However, Jesus tells us not to be so exclusive; we are to open ourselves to the thought that others might have wisdom, ability and truth as well. We might not have God completely sorted out; therefore, we can learn from someone else who sees things a little differently.

Jesus said, 'The one who is not against us is for us,' but, if you flick back a few pages in your Bible, you will find that Jesus said: 'Whoever is not with me is against me' (Matthew 12.30). Is Jesus confused and contradicting himself? Is the Bible always so full of contradictions? Should we just give up and walk away?

WITH US OR AGAINST US?

A point of uncertainty, such as this, is a place where learning can really happen, provided we are willing to engage and tackle it. If we look closely at the passage in Matthew, we can see that some people were dismissing Jesus' work, saying that it was the devil's doing. Jesus' response emphasized that truth is found by holding on to him.

Today's passage from Mark challenges us to consider that, just because we're holding on to Jesus, we don't necessarily have all the answers ourselves. We need one another; we need other followers of Jesus who look, think and behave differently from us, because it helps us to see things another way and to realize that we still have a lot to learn.

There is a tendency towards tribalism in some of us. We judge other Christians with an 'in' or 'out' mentality. We decide whether they are 'real' Christians or not. This behaviour is dangerous because if they are out, then we might be too. Superiority blinds us to our own faults and inhibits self-awareness. We're so convinced that we know better, we'll give no time to other people's ideas and opinions.

Learning from other Christian traditions is important. From church history, we see that when one generation fails to learn from the past, it can become focused on the unimportant and be self-righteous about certain aspects of faith.

I am often asked by people if I am an Anglican. I tend to answer this way:

In my reading of the Bible, I am Evangelical.
In the breaking of bread, I am Catholic.
In the ministry of the Spirit, I am Charismatic.
In the preaching of the gospel, I am Pentecostal.

In serving the poor, I am Franciscan.
When it comes to baptism, I am Baptist.
I think I'm just a Christian.

In other words, I want to learn from anyone wise, good, loving and focused on Jesus. I want to understand why everyone else thinks as they do and why I think as I do. With all this said, we must always check what we learn and think against the Bible because it is the clear foundation that God has given us.

YES, BUT HOW?

When the Bible gets tough, when you have questions about your faith, are you doing any of these things?

- **Holding on to Jesus?** Jesus reveals a God of love who is for us and for everyone willing to turn to him. Don't settle for answers that aren't rooted in him.
- **Going deeper?** Ask difficult questions, wrestle with possible answers, talk to someone you trust. To go deeper, be willing to dig deeper than you have before. Digging deeper means taking the time to ask other Christians questions to understand where they are coming from and why they come to the conclusions that they do.
- **Listening to others?** Talk to someone who might think differently from you. Really listen to him or her. If you read Christian books, try reading a book you think you might disagree with and be open to learning from it. I would recommend doing this under the wisdom and guidance of your own church leaders.

DAY 40
THEREFORE GO

Q. 19: How often do you regularly discuss your faith with others?

Therefore go and make disciples of all nations, baptising them in the name of the Father and of the Son and of the Holy Spirit.
(Matthew 28.19)

There are few things I'm asked more by my fellow Christians than how to talk about faith. It's an area we're often scared of, and one that has to be demystified. Although some are set apart with the specific gift of the evangelist, all who love Jesus need to play their part in witnessing. Nothing will change in the UK if we depend on the odd charismatic personality who can deliver a rousing talk. What we need is something very different. We require a Church that is mobilized, with every single one of us playing our part and stepping into all that the Lord has for us. We all have colleagues, neighbours and friends who the Church may struggle to affect with the good news through any other means than us. God is doing great things and we simply need to play our part and join with him.

The passage from Matthew 28.19 is an interesting one because, locked within the original Greek words, there is some interesting help. In the English, we render *poreuthentes oun* as 'therefore go', but it would probably be more useful to translate it as 'in your going'. In your going to the supermarket, while standing in the queue, travelling on the bus, catching a plane, going to the cinema, chatting with a work friend or visiting a family member be ready to make a disciple. Some people are called to warmer climates for mission and others are called to the street where they live. It's as if Jesus is saying to us, 'Wherever you go today be ready and prepared to give someone what they need to grow a little bit more like me.' What they need might be a word of direction or encouragement, a gift with a note attached, ministering to them in a life-giving way or explaining God's love for them. If you do it – whatever it might be – in Jesus' name, and it helps to bring someone closer to the God who loves them, then you are potentially making a disciple.

YES, BUT HOW?

Here are five quick tips to get you started.

1 **Be interested in others and find things in common** We need to ask questions, show an interest in others and, if or when asked back, take the opportunity to talk about our faith. Alternatively, start by trying to find a point of commonality (a shared hobby, place or something similar). Talk about that area first before bringing up the topic of faith.

2 **Remember that God is with us** As we seek to share our faith with others, we are not alone because the Lord has often gone before us. Let's also remember that the Holy Spirit is at work in people's lives; we are

often building on what he's already started and the input of others.

3 Don't measure success by instant results We need to celebrate the impact we've had when we see progress, no matter how small, and not only when someone finally chooses Jesus.

4 Make it an everyday thing Sharing your faith is like using a muscle. If it's done often, it becomes easier and normal. If not, then the muscle withers away. We should make talking about Jesus as everyday as anything else, and do all we can to open our mouths and speak about our hope in him.

5 Pray We can overestimate our actions and underestimate our prayers. Let's pray for those we want to witness to and for opportunities to do so.

Sharing our faith is not easy but it is vital. How do we start? One word and prayer at a time!

QUESTIONS TO CONSIDER

Think about these questions as you go through your day.

- Where are you going to be today?
- Whom are you going to meet?

SPIRALS

Look at the spiral overleaf. In the centre are the religious places and people. Further out are the somewhat religious places and people. On the outside are the non-religious places and people. With whom are you interacting?

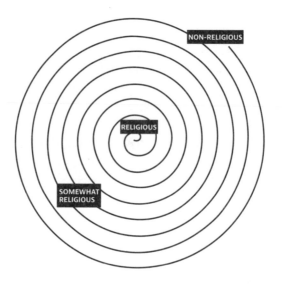

Pray that, today, you will have an opportunity to 'go and make disciples'. Pray that God will equip you to share your faith in the right way and for your eyes to be opened to see people whom you wouldn't usually see.

PRAYER

Lord Jesus Christ, you call us to follow you as disciples.
Help us to respond wholeheartedly without counting the
  cost.

Lord Jesus Christ, you invite us to proclaim your gospel of
  hope and salvation here at home,
  and to all nations and peoples.
Teach us to be faithful evangelists in word and in action.

Lord Jesus Christ, you have given us every spiritual and
  material blessing.
Show us how to share our gifts with others.
Inspire us always to follow your example of generous
  self-giving.

Gracious Lord, teach us to give with joyous and grateful
  hearts.
Help us to provide hope, consolation and pastoral care to
  your people,
  that we may give glory and honour to your holy name.
Amen.

EPILOGUE

THE LORD'S MANIFESTO

Life is an adventure of walking with Jesus, learning from Jesus and then walking *for* Jesus – this book in your hands is only the beginning. Each day brings a new opportunity to be more like him. Jesus gave his followers a powerful manifesto that, as we pray through it, helps us to do just that.

Gathering his followers around himself, Jesus taught them, as he teaches us today, how to pray . . .

> Our Father in heaven,
> holy is your name.
> Your kingdom come;
> your will be done
> on earth as it is in heaven . . .

When we read the Lord's Prayer, it can be all too easy to recount it as a hyper-spiritual transcendent prayer but, for Jesus, it is about the reality of life. For him, there is another world that is possible – it isn't somewhere else; it is right here in the middle of dirt, dust, brick, stone, tower blocks and city landscapes. When he is pushed by Pontius Pilate to explain where his kingdom is, Jesus replied: 'My kingdom is not of this world . . . But now my kingdom is from another place' (John 18.36).

Far from being a prayer that acknowledges that God's going to do what God's going to do, the Lord's Prayer is an act of *rebellion*. As the theologian Tom Wright says, this prayer is a

> risky, crazy prayer of submission and commission, or if you like the prayer of subversion and conversion. It is our way of signing on, in our turn, for the work of the kingdom. It is the way we take the medicine ourselves, so that we may be strong enough to administer it to others. It is the way we retune our instruments to play God's Opera for the world to sing.
> (*The Lord and His Prayer* (SPCK, 2012), p. 12)

BUT WHY IS THIS PRAYER RISKY?

If Jesus' kingdom is from another place, then, when we pray 'Your kingdom come . . . on earth as in heaven', we are actually pledging allegiance to the kingdom of God and not the kingdoms or cultures of this world.

When Jesus first said these words, the disciples knew that they were subject to the empire of Rome and its desire to make them citizens of Rome. The Lord's Prayer, however, was to become a daily reminder that their *true* citizenship is in heaven: not specifically in heaven but in the values and culture of heaven that are coming on earth. The idea of God's kingdom coming to earth is about the very ground we walk on being changed because of the kingdom of God. It's a revolutionary prayer for revolutionary subordination.

BUT WHAT DOES 'REVOLUTIONARY SUBORDINATION' MEAN?

Even though the Lord's Prayer is about submission to another world, another kingdom and another power, Jesus continues to teach about our submitting to earthly authorities. In other words, although we pledge our allegiance to the kingdom of God, we still have to pay our taxes to the government, and pay our water rates and council tax as citizens of the United Kingdom. Even so, Jesus shows us that we can submit to the world while *subverting* it. Indeed, he shows us how the very act of submission is the thing that disarms the powers of darkness by making a spectacle of them. In this way, the Lord's Prayer is a prayer that first encourages us to submit to Jesus and then to be people who subvert the status quo.

The Lord's Prayer is a daily reminder of the kingdom under which we sit. It also gives us an idea of what this kingdom looks like: a place in which there is the daily *provision* of bread from heaven, the practice of *grace* and people faithfully doing what is *right* because evil no longer makes sense.

This prayer was never meant to be said with eyes down and a quiet voice; it is meant to be cried out in pain and longing for more, for a greater heavenly reality on earth, to see God's power cracking open the darkness and oppression of this world. This prayer is meant to be a rebellious rousing of godly revolution.

As you continue to walk in the Way of Rabbi Jesus, walk with this prayer at the heart of all you are and do. Live each day to bring the culture of heaven to earth, forgive others, live with grace, direct your life away from the evil one and live for the kingdom of God.